ALSO BY KEN LIU

THE DANDELION DYNASTY

The Grace of Kings

The Wall of Storms

The Veiled Throne

Speaking Bones

The Paper Menagerie and Other Stories

The Hidden Girl and Other Stories

LAOZI'S DAO DE JING

A NEW INTERPRETATION
FOR A TRANSFORMATIVE TIME

KEN LIU

SCRIBNER

New York Amsterdam/Antwerp London Toronto Sydney New Delhi

Scribner

An Imprint of Simon & Schuster, LLC

1230 Avenue of the Americas

New York, NY 10020

First Scribner trade paperback edition January 2025

SCRIBNER and design are trademarks of Simon & Schuster, LLC

For information about special discounts for bulk purchases,
please contact Simon & Schuster Special Sales at 1-866-506-1949
or business@simonandschuster.com.

The Simon & Schuster Speakers Bureau can bring authors to
your live event. For more information or to book an event,
contact the Simon & Schuster Speakers Bureau at 1-866-248-3049
or visit our website at www.simonspeakers.com.

Interior design by Kyle Kabel

Manufactured in the United States of America

1   3   5   7   9   10   8   6   4   2

Library of Congress Cataloging-in-Publication Data is available.

ISBN 978-1-6680-1936-8
ISBN 978-1-6680-1937-5 (pbk)
ISBN 978-1-6680-1938-2 (ebook)

PART I

THE BOOK
OF DAO

Chapter 1

THE GATE TO WONDER

The path that can be walked is not the path that lasts; the
name that can be spoken is not the name that endures.
Nothingness, the origin of heaven and earth; presence, the
mother of all creation.
Empty the mind of desire, so you can take in Dao's marvels.
Fill the mind with will, so you can discern Dao's frontier.
This pair of diverging names flow from the same source,
both descriptions of mystery, the mystery of mysteries,
the gate to wonder.

Not Quite an Introduction

Most books begin with introductions, but in this one, I've deliberately put what passes for an "introduction" after the first chapter.

I promise why I've done this will soon become clear.

The first chapter of Laozi's *Dao De Jing* (sometimes called the *Book of the Way and Its Virtue*) contains what is likely the most famous passage from the whole book. Many people who know nothing else about Daoism have heard some version of it. Indeed, some think that the entirety of Laozi's philosophy is encapsulated within it.

> The path that can be walked is not the path that lasts;
> the name that can be spoken is not the name that endures.

It feels like exactly the right quote to start a book about finding a path of tranquility through a turbulent world.

But what if I told you that this quote isn't, in fact, the first chapter?

In the early 1970s, in a place called Mawangdui, which is in the heart of Hunan Province, a region rich with history since the earliest days of Chinese civilization, archaeologists excavated a set of tombs belonging to nobles who lived during the second century before the Common Era. The excavation revealed many rare artifacts, including some of the earliest surviving manuscripts of the *Dao De Jing*. (Yes, *manuscripts*—two versions, written on silk scrolls, were found at Mawangdui.)

Compared to the received text of the *Dao De Jing* that most readers in subsequent eras have studied, the Mawangdui versions contain many subtle as well as startling differences. The biggest difference of all is that what we think of as the Book of De, or the second part of the *Dao De Jing*, is at the beginning of the Mawangdui versions. The Book of Dao, or what we think of as the first part of the *Dao De Jing*, instead comes at the end. (The Mawangdui scrolls weren't even titled the *Dao De Jing*, but simply "Five Thousand Words from Laozi.") This first chapter, therefore, sits right at the middle of the whole book, not the start.

And even the Mawangdui scrolls aren't *the* earliest known versions of the *Dao De Jing*. That honor belongs to fragmentary bamboo slips discovered in a tomb in a place called Guodian, a few hundred kilometers to the north of Mawangdui, and excavated in 1993, dating to some time in the fourth century before the Common Era. Written using a beautiful script specific to the state of Chu during the Warring States period, the bamboo slips predate the Mawangdui text by more than a century. The slips don't follow the organization of either the Mawangdui text or the subsequent received text and appear to be a compilation spanning some years.

Some have called the Mawangdui and Guodian texts more "authentic," more "authoritative," supposedly free from the intervention of later copyists and editors. But I don't find that idea helpful. Even the Mawangdui and Guodian versions were written centuries after the *Dao De Jing* was first composed, and the received text, having accumulated millennia's worth of commentary and informed the understanding of generations of readers and thinkers, has an authority of its own.

As a writer myself, I'm keenly aware of the instability of texts and the futility of tracing and enforcing authority. Each of my published pieces of fiction exists in multiple versions and contains alterations made during transmission and publication: typos and editorial interventions sometimes become canon; corrections I make don't get to press on time; first publications and revisions compete for attention; even my preferred, "final" versions are often displaced by translations and abridgments and excerpts and pirated copies and even censored editions. Not a single story or novel I've ever written has been published 100 percent in the exact form I wanted. Literally no "authoritative" version of my fiction exists anywhere except in my head. And when I die, it will be gone; only the tangible, nonauthoritative texts will remain.

But this is true of every single piece of writing that has ever been disseminated and become embodied in multiple copies. Moreover, the text, as a string of symbols, is not the locus of meaning—understanding comes at the moment when a reader's mind fills the text with their own language of experience and expectation and transforms the dead text into a living story, one unique to them and them alone. All readings are translations, edits, emendations, corrections, rewritings—there is no other way.

Thus, *authenticity* and *authoritative* are always loaded terms that tell us more about those who would like to claim the power of judgment than about reality.

> Nothingness, the origin of heaven and earth; presence, the
>   mother of all creation.
> Empty the mind of desire, so you can take in Dao's marvels.
> Fill the mind with will, so you can discern Dao's frontier.

The more helpful approach, I think, is to remember Laozi's general contempt for obsession with language, with mere shadows and tracks instead of living wisdom itself. Whether a chapter comes at the beginning or the end or the middle doesn't matter, for there is no beginning nor end nor middle to Dao itself.

That is why, while I have consulted the Mawangdui and Guodian texts, I don't treat them as any more authoritative than the received text, and I have not altered the traditional order of the chapters.

I hope we have more discoveries like Mawangdui and Guodian in the future, so that we can have more tracks and shadows and traces to study—however, the ultimate blessing is not to find more texts, but to feel closer to Dao.

*　　*　　*

The instability of the text of the *Dao De Jing* is why I've decided to put the introduction after the first chapter, and I've scattered such things as timelines, notes, a biography of Laozi, parables, observations—things conventionally relegated to appendices—throughout the text. I don't think Laozi particularly cared about following conventions, and sometimes only by throwing away the map can we find the way.

Now, then, to the introduction proper. Laozi's book, written two and a half millennia ago, needs no introduction. But *this* particular version seems to beg for one. Many, many editions of the *Dao De Jing* are available in English already; so, why another one?

I could answer this question by pointing out flaws in existing translations; I could emphasize my own strength and perspective as a bicultural writer; I could tell you about the difference between translations done by those born inside the culture of the source text and those coming at it from outside; I could give you a manifesto on translation philosophy; I could tell you about the impact of history and the colonial gaze, and how everything fits into structures of power so that no translation is ever neutral; I could speak to you about personal resistance and cultural decolonization and reclaiming a literary heritage—

I stop here because none of that matters, not to me, not to you, and most certainly not to Laozi.

Of all the philosophers who have ever held the esteem of billions around the globe, Laozi is the humblest and also the most elusive. Whereas Zhuangzi, the fellow Daoist with whom Laozi is often closely associated, showed flashes of impatience and arrogance, Laozi never, ever lost his cool. He writes like the flow of water—all-encompassing, always-yielding, never-pressing, ever-doubting. Core to his philosophy is the idea that the fool is wiser than the self-proclaimed clever man, that trying to prove a point is never as good as simply living the truth, that striving and contending and vying for dominance are counterproductive—the best way to silence those who doubt you is by not playing their game.

In the *Dao De Jing*, Laozi doesn't see the need to justify himself, to anticipate counterarguments, to furnish syllogisms to dress up his insights about the cosmos with a patina of human rationality. Why should those who translate him feel any more need to justify themselves, to convince you to listen?

So I will explain myself only when it pleases me to, and all my decisions are my own, not anyone else's. I won't pepper this translation with footnotes and glossaries; I won't parade before you a list of scholars, ancient and modern, in some misguided effort to borrow their authority for myself; I won't lay out my arguments about the technical and aesthetic aspects of translation in anticipation of my critics.

These things smack of trying to prove cleverness, to display credentials, to show off—all antithetical to the Daoist view of life. Trying to justify a perspective, no matter how well-intentioned the effort, is resistance, contention, assertion, aggression, dominance. We may have been taught by modernity that these qualities are always desirable and universally good, but the truth is otherwise. They are especially not helpful in a conversation with the *Dao De Jing*.

Instead, I will tell you a story.

It was the middle of the pandemic; months had passed since I last wrote a word. I had never run out of stories since the age of five. But here I was, taleless.

My work was to tell stories about the future, futures brought about by the work of humans, a species that is by no means perfect but whose efforts to perfect itself I held as an article of faith.

The pandemic, however, destroyed that faith. The disease itself didn't scare me, but the politics did. All around me I saw saber-rattling, finger-pointing, paranoia, jostling for power, calls for war. Lies were the most popular stories, varieties of hate the loudest voices, acts of violence the most memorable deeds.

Nations and peoples of the world did not come together as one when an existential threat faced all humanity. Instead, they viewed it as a perfect opportunity to divide, to conquer, to fall apart.

Someone who ought to know better wrote an article celebrating the high death toll in our country as a sign that we were ready for war. Someone else who ought to know better wrote an article musing that Americans of Asian descent were perhaps not "American" enough.

All of a sudden, I no longer felt home in my country.

It was impossible to tell stories about the future. It was also impossible to read stories written by others—those other stories took place in a world before the pandemic; they didn't account for *this*.

For solace I tried to escape into things that weren't storytelling. I fixed old video game consoles, running my soldering iron up and down the ribbon cable, seeing the dead screen slowly coming back to life as the aged solder, refreshed by the heat, allowed electricity to flow across dry contacts once again. I baked bread, losing myself in kneading and folding, much as Ishmael loses himself on the *Pequod* squeezing the lumps in whale spermaceti. I trained neural networks, feeding them my own fiction in the hope—not entirely unserious— that a robot version of my mind could go on to tell stories about the future while I no longer could.

And I began to read the *Dao De Jing*.

In the millennia since its composition, Laozi's book has become an integral part of Chinese cultures and languages. It is the source of countless allusions, metaphors, fixed expressions, idioms. To grow up Chinese was to absorb Laozi through the very air. I knew that governing a country was no different from cooking a small fish. I knew that the best vessels would come out of the kiln last. I knew that the ideal political state involved some aphorism about roosters crowing and dogs barking. I knew that these bits came from Laozi even though I had never read the *Dao De Jing*, in the same way that I could hold up a plastic skull and proclaim

"Alas, poor Yorick!" as a kid long before I read any Shake-speare.

But I had never read the book from start to finish. Like many other classics, I simply assumed I knew it through its translations, quotations, fixed expressions, dead metaphors.

In desperation, I began to read the *Dao De Jing*. I read it because I could no longer read or tell stories. I read it because the future seemed absolutely hopeless. I read it hoping to find a way out of the darkness.

And it was nothing like I expected. In the *Dao De Jing*, Laozi is not the kind and wise sage of Orientalist fairy tales, spewing platitudes that say nothing. He's sharp but doesn't cut; he's righteous but doesn't judge; he's hopeful but not sweet.

> The root of lightness is weight;
> The master of recklessness is repose.
> Why does a lord of ten thousand chariots treat the fate of
>   the world so lightly?

Sometimes his words can seem like clichés, but that's only because they're so embedded in our collective conscious-ness. Sometimes he can come across as a provocateur, almost trolling, but that's because he doesn't think language itself makes much sense.

> If it's not laughed at, it isn't worthy of being Dao.
> The advancing Dao appears to retreat;
> The straight Dao appears twisted.

Laozi doesn't comfort. He doesn't persuade. He doesn't offer solace.

> Heaven and earth are not benevolent. To them, all things in
> the cosmos are straw dogs.
> The Dao-aware are not benevolent. To them, the people
> are straw dogs.

He simply makes observations about Dao, the path of providence, of grace, of life itself. There's no need for Laozi to convince you of anything, for he's not trying to sell you anything. You can take his words or leave them; it's all the same to him.

Instead, he invites the reader to have a conversation with his text, through which the readers must discover their own way. The text is not what matters, but the attempt to see the shimmering water flowing beyond the channels of the text. Again and again, Laozi insists, Dao cannot be taught; you must come to it yourself.

In that refusal to confront, to judge, to direct, Laozi did comfort me, persuade me, give me solace. What can be more comforting than to have a conversation with a mind that has transcended mortality, a voice that has survived the ages?

> Between heaven and earth is a bellows, empty but inexhaust-
> ible. The more movement, the more powerful the flow.

The more I read, the more I wanted to argue, to contend, to dispute, and then, later, to yield, to accept, to imagine. In that conversation with Laozi's text, I began to see the shape of my own life, the questions that opened seams, the patterns that pooled and shimmered. I began to feel the desire to write again—though that would have to wait for another book.

It wasn't a way out, not yet, but a path always began with the desire to walk.

Meanwhile, a record of my conversation with him could be set down, which might be more conventionally termed a translation. All translations are, ultimately, a record of the translator's trials to discern the spirit of the text within its shadowy mirror. This translation merely makes that struggle obvious instead of hiding it, a foolish honesty that I think Laozi would appreciate.

That is how this book came to be.

After hundreds of generations, a single tomb in Hunan Province could transform the way we understand the textual order of the *Dao De Jing*. Who's to say that after thousands of translations, this one won't touch you in a way that others haven't?

In the end, a dandelion needs no reason to blossom, even though a thousand other flowers are already blooming. A child needs no rationale to sing, even though a thousand other songs have already been sung. I need no rationale to produce a new translation of the *Dao De Jing* other than to declare that I love the book and wish to do so.

As I mentioned, Daoists in general do not think we should obsess over words and texts—they are like footprints and shadows, mere dead traces by aid of which we're supposed to discover the living truth, which is impossible to capture using mere language. Yet, language remains the only, flawed technology through which we can attempt this search for the truth, this struggle for meaning. This is the central paradox of not just translation and communication, but the very means by which we construct our transcendent selves through imperfect language.

Laozi's text, open-ended, playful, multivalent, so artful that it appears uncrafted, poses particular difficulties for translators. Taking to heart Laozi's admonition not to be "clever," in this translation I've deliberately tried to be plain and direct, forsaking erudition for clarity. I don't strain to imitate the original's wordplay or strive to approximate the purposeful ambiguity in Laozi's classical Chinese formulations—trying to do so has been the downfall of far too many translators. Because choosing what not to say is far more important than choosing what to say, I prefer to present a simple sketch that captures what I find most striking in the original rather than a messy painting that tries to encompass everything, thereby catching nothing.

A plain translation strives for the Daoist ideal of uncarved wood, eschewing ornamentation and ostentatious craft. A plain translation, however, does not *simplify*. Laozi does not present Dao in straightforward, simplified language, with sentences that pose no challenge to the reader, through metaphors that don't demand the reader to think. This is because sentences that require no effort from the reader to understand are the most *artificial*, for they hew closest to the conventions, clichés, and fashions of society. Paradoxically, to shock the reader into lasting reflection, to guide the listener into discovering the eternal nature of Dao for themselves, Laozi must use language that is purposefully unconventional, unusual, unsmooth.

"The straight Dao appears twisted," as Laozi says.

Like Laozi's original, a plain translation yearns to be like the uncarved branch. An uncarved branch is full of knots and burrs, forks and bends, unexpected turns that force the mind to seek new patterns; it's covered in rough bark that scrapes away the calluses of the banal and trivial, that scratches at the raw nerves of our cocooned mind, lulled into complacency by the varnish of unquestioned modernity; it isn't smooth and easy.

I avoided certain clichés in English translations of Chinese classics, such as the use of "gentlemen" and "sage" for *jūnzǐ* and *shèngrén*, respectively. In the same way that derivatives and imitations can get in the way of our raw encounter with the classics, these clichés, products of another time, get in the way of the understanding of the contemporary reader. In places where Laozi's words may appear out of step with modern sentiment, I chose to leave them alone rather than rewriting, for I think it better for the reader to form their own rehabilitative interpretations, if they wish, rather than for me to impose one on them. I also declined to adopt a pseudo-verse form, as Laozi's original is poetic, but not formal poetry. Laozi preferred the beauty of nature to craft, and so I feel the plain rhythm of everyday English prose, stripped of the artifice intended to show off the craft of the translator, suits the text best.

In a few places where I made specific translation decisions that seem notable and where an explanation may add to the reader's conversation with the text, I've added a brief note to elaborate.

The biggest obstacle to full engagement with the *Dao De Jing* is the temptation to rush through. The chapters are so short, so "simple," that the modern reader, trained from toddlerhood to "consume" content, to race to the end of the paragraph before it has scrolled off the screen, to scan for "main ideas" rather than to let each and every word fill the mind, is tempted to finish it in twenty minutes. If you try that approach, you will certainly consume the *Dao De Jing*, but I won't agree that you've read it.

To counter that temptation, I've supplemented the translation with some parables by Zhuangzi, another Daoist master whose fantastic tales have illuminated the *Dao De Jing* for generations of readers. The stories give the text texture, more places for the mind to find purchase, more nooks and crannies to explore. These stories aren't included to "illustrate" specific points; rather, I've put them in places where the flow of the conversation feels right to me.

More knowledge brings fewer paths; better to keep hollow, stay open.

May you keep hollow and stay open.

Chapter 2

WITHOUT BEAUTY

Because beauty is acknowledged by all as beautiful, ugliness
springs into being.

Because goodness is recognized by all as good, evil has
meaning.

Presence and absence give birth to each other; difficult and
easy complete each other; long and short complement
each other; high and low fulfill each other; sound and
syllable harmonize each other; before and after order
each other; always.

This is why the Dao-aware do by not doing and teach without speaking.

They let the world flourish without intrusion.

Create without possessing, give without expecting, achieve
without credit.

By laying no claim, the Dao-aware make the work last.

Chapter 3

DO BY NOT DOING

By not prizing talent, they remove the appetite for competition.

By not valuing the rare, they eliminate the inclination to steal.

By not flaunting the desirable, they calm the hearts of the people.

The Dao-aware govern by emptying minds, filling bellies, weakening ambitions, strengthening bones, sustaining all in the freedom from knowing, from desiring, so that even the crafty dare not act.

Do by not doing, and there is nothing that cannot be done.

Laozi's Life

All texts are defined by, as well as transcend, the times they are written in. To make sense of the *Dao De Jing*, it helps to know a little about the era of its composition.

Compared to Egypt, Mesopotamia, Greece, or Rome, ancient classical Chinese civilization (by which I mean prior to the founding of the Qin Dynasty in the year 221 before the Common Era) has left relatively few surviving texts to subsequent ages (the *Dao De Jing*, thankfully, is one of them). Grand discoveries such as the Mawangdui and Guodian sites are all too rare. The reasons for this paucity of texts are many, but at least one cause is the constant warfare among the various small Sinophone states that would eventually unify into China.

The era between the eighth and third centuries BCE, when these states nominally were vassals of the king of Zhou, was further subdivided into the Spring and Autumn period and the Warring States period—that latter name alone should tell you all you need to know about this chaotic time. As the Bronze Age gradually gave way to the Iron Age, grand lords raised armies of tens of thousands of men and thousands of chariots, contending for hegemony over the flat plains and fertile river valleys, razing cities and slaughtering captives. Interminable warfare brought incredible suffering to the people as well as destruction of texts, artifacts, buildings, art. This state of affairs would not abate until the conquest of all the other states by Qin in 221 BCE.

As thinkers tried to make sense of the deaths all around them and sought refuge from, or new paths out of, the unceasing instability, the era also witnessed the great flowering of classical Chinese philosophy. Writers and orators developed schools of thought such as Confucianism (emphasis on benevolence and humanism), Legalism (emphasis on efficient administration and realpolitik), Mohism (emphasis on all-encompassing love and empiricism), and many others.

One of these was Daoism (or "the philosophy of the way"), for which the *Dao De Jing* is a founding text. I don't think I'm spoiling the rest of the book by telling you that it is about *Dao*, or the Way, which is, among other things, a way out of chaos, warfare, pain, and into harmony, peace, joy.

As you converse with the text, it's impossible not to sense the shadow cast over every page by the history of those warring states.

When Laozi speaks of "a lord of ten thousand chariots," it isn't a *mere* stock phrase. When Laozi writes about mares being forced to deliver foals on the battlefield, it isn't *only* an emotionally powerful image. When he goes on and on about risks and threats and death and loss, they aren't abstractions, not at all.

By not prizing talent, they remove the appetite for competition.
By not valuing the rare, they eliminate the inclination to steal.
By not flaunting the desirable, they calm the hearts of the people.

To understand the full import of these pleas, you have to remember the suffering brought about by the ambition of grand lords and the pride of great states—terrors that humanity in the modern era has only too much experience of, even if those living in the "developed world" have mostly been shielded from the consequences of policies pursued on their behalf in distant lands against victims who cannot vote in the developed world's elections.

Laozi was writing at a time of great invention and technological and social change, when everyone fumbled in the dark for the emergence of a new world order, when grand lords celebrated war and wise counselors fretted about hegemony and vassalage, when beauty contended with terror, chaos danced with cleverness, and the world was rocked by grand theories and petty rivalries, and the way through the dark wood, for individuals as well as nations, seemed impossibly obscure.

Doesn't sound all that different from our time, does it?

One consequence of the relative paucity of texts from Laozi's time is that we don't know much about him. (*Laozi* is not a name but more like a nickname that expresses affection as well as honor—something like "elder teacher.")

This lack of biographical information is true of many great thinkers from that era, such as Laozi's fellow Daoist Zhuangzi. But whereas Zhuangzi comes across vividly as a figure in his own parables, giving you a clear sense of his personality, Laozi is self-effacing in the *Dao De Jing*, his voice dissolving into the text like the fading cry of a loon over a New England lake long after the bird has departed.

We're not even sure exactly when he lived during those centuries of constant warfare. In some accounts he is a contemporary of Confucius, which would place his life sometime in the sixth century before the Common Era. But some think he is a contemporary of Zhuangzi, who lived in the fourth century before the Common Era (this would be around the time of Plato, an equally great but very different sort of philosopher).

Much of what we think we know about Laozi's life isn't from contemporaneous accounts, but a brief biography written at least two hundred years (and perhaps as many as five hundred years) later. Sima Qian, the first systematic historian of China, composed a short biography that combined the lives of four Chinese philosophers: Laozi, Zhuangzi, Shenzi, and Hanfeizi.

(This is a curious combination to modern eyes. Sima Qian combined these figures from different times into one entry because he saw in them a continuity of ideas. But Laozi and Zhuangzi, being Daoists, thought the fewer laws the better, whereas Shenzi and Hanfeizi, being Legalists, thought the entire point of government was to intervene and intervene some more. To put them together requires too much cleverness to be plausible to me, so I shall say no more about that.)

According to Sima Qian, Laozi was born in the State of Chu (in today's Henan Province). His given name was Li Er, courtesy name Dan, and he worked as an archive keeper for the court of Zhou.

To give a character sketch of Laozi, Sima Qian tells the following story about an encounter between him and Confucius, the great sage and founder of Confucianism:

On his way to the capital, Confucius stopped to ask Laozi for advice.

Laozi said to him, "You are teaching the words of dead sages, whose bones have rotted away, leaving only empty echoes. When circumstances align, a wise person can look forward to becoming a minister in the palace, free to fulfill their vision like a horse given space to run, but when luck doesn't go their way, a wise person will have to tumble with the wind like a clump of weed by the side of the road. I've heard that a good merchant conceals their treasures and goods so that they appear to have nothing, and a wise person focuses on building up their own virtue while appearing foolish and lowly. You should abandon your pride and prune your appetites, for fame and ambition are not good for you. That is all I have to tell you."

After Confucius returned to his students, he said, "I know that a bird can fly, a fish can swim, and a beast can prance about. The prancing I can snare in a net; the swimming I can hook with a line; the flying I can shoot with an arrow. But a dragon . . . I have no idea what to do, for a dragon can ride the wind to be among clouds. Today I saw a dragon among mere men."

Stories like this one, starring Confucius and Laozi, are popular and offer in parable form the contrast between their philosophies. You'll encounter a few more like it in this book.

In a move that rather reminds me of Herodotus's fantastic "I'm just writing down what I heard" stories, Sima Qian adds, "Some say that Laozi lived to be a hundred and sixty, and some say two hundred. His longevity was the result of his cultivation of Dao."

Sima Qian also tells a story about Laozi and his one and only book, which I quote in its entirety here:

Laozi studied Dao and De, and his philosophy directed the practitioner to retreat from the secular world, shunning fame. As he foresaw the inevitable decline of the Zhou court, he decided to follow his philosophy and depart. Once he reached Hangu Pass, the guard there, Yinxi, said to him, "Master, since you're about to leave the secular world behind, please write down your teachings." That is how Laozi ended up composing a book divided into two parts, consisting of about five thousand characters. As for where he wandered to once he was through the pass, nobody knows.

As we know from the Mawangdui and Guodian texts, this book is the *Dao De Jing*.

There are many theories about Laozi: that he didn't exist, that he actually lived after Zhuangzi, that he was a legendary figure conflated from multiple real people (and the *Dao De Jing* is thus a compilation of Daoist teachings by other authors), and so on. The debate over these things can get quite heated.

Like most things that clever scholars argue about, I think you can ignore them. It's enough to know that the *Dao De Jing* was composed during a time of great turmoil and change, that it embodies a soul who sought and found wisdom, that it asks nothing of those who converse with it other than a willingness to listen, to find their own way.

Chapter 4

A VESSEL FROM WHICH THE FLOW NEVER ENDS

Dao is a vessel from which the flow never ends.

Unfathomable! Like the origin of all things.

Dulling edges, dissolving entanglements, hiding glows, fusing
with terrestrial dust, it fades away . . . or does it?

I know not from what it descends. Maybe it's older than
the Creator.

The Wheelwright and
the Limits of Language

The description of Dao in this chapter exemplifies the mysticism in some of Laozi's writing.

Dulling edges, dissolving entanglements, hiding glows, fusing with terrestrial dust—the terms are deliberately vague, opaque, ambivalent, confusing. There are a thousand other ways to translate them into English, and none of them would be any clearer.

Laozi wrote this way because he wanted to emphasize that language is ultimately a misleading guide. We think that when something is nameable, it is real, but "the name that can be spoken is not the name that endures." Conversely, we think what cannot be spoken about does not exist, but the most important knowledge is never reducible to words.

Speaking of the limits of language, I'm reminded of a story from Zhuangzi about Duke Huan, one of the most powerful princes during the time when the petty Chinese states were at war, a true lord of ten thousand chariots, and his humble wheelwright.

(Oh, one more thing: Reader, as a general rule, I won't be translating the parables from Zhuangzi literally. I'll retell them as needed to suit the purpose of making your conversation with Laozi more interesting.)

One day, as Duke Huan read in the great hall of his palace, he nodded and exclaimed by turns.

An old wheelwright named Bian was carving wheels in the yard outside the hall. His curiosity piqued by the duke's excited cries, the old man put down his mallet and chisel and climbed the steps into the hall.

"Sire, what are you reading?" he asked.

"The words of sages," replied the duke.

"Are these sages still alive?"

"No. They died a long time ago."

The wheelwright was disappointed. "Then what you're reading is nothing more than ancient dregs."

"How dare you!" the duke roared. "I'm conversing with the greatest minds in history, but you, a mere maker of wheels, think that you can judge the worth of far nobler minds. Explain!"

The wheelwright bowed to the angry duke but answered without fear. "I speak only from my low station and ordinary experience. Sire, do you know how to carve a wheel?"

The duke gazed through the portico into the yard, where the wheelwright had left his tools and half-finished wheels. The idea of fashioning a wheel out of wood seemed clear enough.

The wheelwright went on, "If you hew slowly and broadly, the cuts will be smooth but the wheel won't be sturdy. But if you carve quickly in small steps, then the chisel won't bite true and the wheel will be too rough. To make a proper wheel, you have to study the tendency of the lumber and feel the flow in the grain, know the purposes of different vehicles and the variations in their construction, understand how a wheel rim wears down differently in summer versus winter, against mud versus sand.

"Above all, you have to learn to wield the tools as though they were extensions of your mind and to chip at a steady pace, neither too fast nor too slow, neither too heavy nor too light."

The duke considered the wheelwright's words, nodding slowly.

The wheelwright continued, "But all this I learned through my hands. My knowledge cannot be captured in words, even though there is a lifetime of art in each swing of the mallet, a career of practice in each placement of the chisel. I cannot teach my son what I know no matter how long I talk, and he cannot learn the soul of my craft no matter how hard he listens. That is why, even though I'm already seventy, I'm still here making wheels myself."

The duke looked from the wheelwright to the book in his hand, then from the book in his hand back to the wheelwright.

The wheelwright nodded. "The ancients died along with their wisdom, wisdom that also cannot be caught by mere words. The shadows on that page are just that, shadows."

As commentary on the parable, Zhuangzi also writes:

People all over the world treasure books. Books are valuable because of the words contained in them, and words are valued for the meaning that they can express. However, the meaning that can be discerned from the words are mere trails, left behind by what cannot be expressed. People make books because they value words, but I think words are not themselves worthy.

What can be seen are mere forms and colors; what can be heard are mere names and syllables. How sad! So many think that forms, colors, names, and syllables are enough to get at reality.

Those who speak, don't know, and those who know, don't speak. A simple matter really, but so hard to fathom.

Chapter 5

STRAW DOGS

Heaven and earth are not benevolent. To them, all things in
the cosmos are straw dogs.

The Dao-aware are not benevolent. To them, the people
are straw dogs.

Between heaven and earth is a bellows, empty but inexhaust-
ible. The more movement, the more powerful the flow.

More knowledge brings fewer paths; better to keep hollow,
stay open.

Nightmares

This chapter contains some of the most striking imagery in the *Dao De Jing*.

What are straw dogs, and what do they have to do with the cosmos?

For help, let's turn to Zhuangzi, where we find that in ancient times, long before the time of Laozi, dogs made of straw were used as offerings to the gods after the custom of live sacrifices faded away. Before the ceremony, the straw dogs would be endowed with the highest of honors, draped in silk and stored in bamboo baskets, paraded in front of all. After the ceremony, they would be discarded as so much trash, trampled on by departing worshippers and stuffed into stoves as cooking fuel.

Imagine, Zhuangzi writes, if we took the discarded straw dogs after the ceremony and wrapped them afresh in patterned silk, stored them once more in bamboo baskets, and placed them again in sacred temples, wouldn't the straw dogs suffer endless nightmares?

The living are crushed mercilessly every day by the vicissitudes of nature. Predators eat their prey alive. Out of thousands born, a few survive to maturity. Providence's bounty is matched only by its cruelty and arbitrariness. All life is a dance of terror and beauty.

Heaven and earth do not care about us; the universe is, ultimately, too grand, too inhumanly scaled.

How then to retain meaning at the human scale, to feel at one with the movement of the stars even as we love and laugh and cry and give birth and fade away? That is the only question worth asking in all philosophy.

> Between heaven and earth is a bellows, empty but inexhaust-
> ible. The more movement, the more powerful the flow.

Chapter 6

SPIRIT OF THE GORGE

Deathless spirit of the gorge, called the ineffable feminine.
The gate of birth, called the root of earth and heaven.
Ever-flowing, never-ceasing, an imperceptible presence.
Use it. It cannot be used up.

Chapter 7

SELFLESS SELF

Heaven abides; earth endures.

Without struggling to preserve themselves, they last.

The Dao-aware put themselves last and so transcend competition, disregard the ego and so preserve their person.

By acting selflessly, do they not therefore realize the self?

The Dao-Aware

The term *shèngrén* is often rendered as "sage" in translations of the Chinese classics. For the *Dao De Jing*, I've chosen to use the term *Dao-aware* instead. Similarly, instead of rendering *yǒudàozhě* as "those in possession of Dao," I also use the term the *Dao-aware*.

To me, *sage* implies a higher status than that of commoners, but I don't think Laozi thought Daoists have higher status—if anything, they're lower, being closer to the nature of water. Likewise, I don't see how Dao can be "possessed" by anyone. The term *yǒudàozhě* really means someone who has found the right path and is following it with joy.

I think *Dao-aware* gets closest to what Laozi is trying to say in this passage. To be a Daoist is to become ever more aware of the patterns of the eternal flux between heaven and earth, the dance of terror and beauty.

Empty the mind of desire, so you can take in Dao's marvels.
Fill the mind with will, so you can discern Dao's frontier.

Chapter 8

WATER

The highest form of good is like water.
By nourishing everything without strife and flowing to places
    that the multitudes disdain, water comes nearest to Dao.
In living, good is to be close to the earth.
In mind, good is to be an echoing gorge.
In society, good is to be kind.
In speech, good is to be true to your word.
In governance, good is to be tidy.
In work, good is to be capable.
In action, good is to be timely.
By not contending, there can be no error.

The Character of Water

I like the gloss given to this chapter by Wang Anshi, a prominent scholar and reformer of the eleventh century of the Common Era, whose comments on Laozi I find particularly illuminating.

In Wang Anshi's note on this chapter, he elucidates how all of Laozi's examples of the manifestation of Dao are drawn from the behavior of water.

"In living, good is to be close to the earth."
Water flows to the lowest elevation.
"In mind, good is to be an echoing gorge."
Water in deep pools is still.
"In society, good is to be kind."
Water gives to all and nourishes all, without expectation
   of return.
"In speech, good is to be true to your word."
Water may take a thousand turns along the way, but you
   can trust it will always flow into the sea.
"In governance, good is to be tidy."

The gentlest force, by constancy and repetition, can triumph
over the strongest obstacle.
"In work, good is to be capable."
Water can take the shape of any vessel, be it square or round.
"In action, good is to be timely."
In spring, water carries; in winter, ice supports.

Chapter 9

SEEDS OF COLLAPSE

Pouring into a bowl already brimming ends with a spill.
Grinding a blade already keen knicks and rolls the edge.
Heaped treasure cannot be kept for long.
Pride from success sows the seeds of collapse.
To retire after a task done well is Dao.

Pao Ding Carving Cattle

A man named Pao Ding was carving beef cattle in front of King Hui of Wei. As Pao Ding danced around the carcass, his hands roaming, feet shuffling, knees flexing, shoulders bracing, turning the knife this way and that, the music of the slithering blade separating flesh from bone filled the air, like a virtuoso plucking at a zither.

The king was amazed. "How did you become so skilled?"

Pao Ding stopped and turned to the king. "When I first began carving cattle as an apprentice, all I could see was the body of the whole animal, an undifferentiated mass. Later, as a journeyman, I no longer saw cattle, but parts working in harmony like components in an intricate engine. Now, with years of experience behind me, I don't rely on my eyes anymore, but carve by touch. I guide the tip of the blade along the natural shape of the animal's body, finding seams and openings between bone and flesh, separating one from the other without application of force. I never even have to saw through tendons, let alone hack at bones. An ordinary butcher changes his blade once a month, for his knife is often forced to hew against bone. A skilled butcher, on the other hand, needs to change his blade but once a year, for his knife cuts nothing but flesh."

"What about you?" asked the king. "How often do you change your blade?"

"I've been using this knife"—Pao Ding held up his tool—"for nineteen years. I've carved thousands of cows with it, but the edge is still as keen as the day I last took it to the grindstone. When I get to parts of the carcass where tendons and bones come together in a knotty mess, I move deliberately and concentrate hard, feel for the tiny openings into which I can insert the tip of my knife, widen them into seams, and then glide the edge in between, separating this from that, until I pull the knife out and the flesh sloughs off the bones like a collapsing heap of earth.

"Then I stand up straight and look around—there's no feeling better in the world. Quickly, I clean the knife and put it away."

"Thank you," said the king. "Now I understand the secret to a good life."

As is the case with most parables from Zhuangzi, this story is capable of many interpretations.

Like Bian the wheelwright's skill, Pao Ding's skill in carving cattle can only be felt, not taught via words. No matter how flowery the description, no one can replicate his feat by reading alone. The words are mere tracks, empty traces left by the elusive truth.

Often, this story is interpreted as an illustration of the flow of Dao itself: like Pao Ding's knife, Dao takes on the character of water, seeks openings and seams, follows the natural shape of the world to go from where it is to where it isn't. What is prized is not confrontation, force, dominance, hacking at the problem like a butcher of ordinary skill, but patience, insight, acceptance, to overcome by not contending, to do by not doing.

I bring up this story here, however, to draw your attention to the final lines:

> Then I stand up straight and look around—there's no feeling better in the world. Quickly, I clean the knife and put it away.

Pao Ding acknowledges the joy of a task done well—he looks around, proud of his achievement, but only for a moment. Immediately he cleans the knife and puts it away, not just to protect the blade, but also to leave no trace that he has done the deed.

I think far too little attention has been paid to the way Zhuangzi ends this story, even though that's the part that inspires the king (and us as well). It's perfectly okay to take pride in your work, to celebrate it, even, for a moment, but the only way to make that joy last is to retire immediately, to not insist on overstaying the moment.

A full moon can only wane; from the peak of the mountain there's nowhere to go but down.

Chapter 10

INEFFABLE DE

Can you fuse your soul with flesh—becoming one without partition?

Can you gather your breath into tenderness—turning once more into a newborn?

Can you cleanse the mirror of your spirit—reflecting pure light?

Can you love the people and serve the country—doing so by not doing?

Can you open yourself to your senses—quieting the mind like water?

Can you pierce your consciousness—opening new paths until you know nothing?

To birth, to nourish, to create without possessing, to give without expecting, to nurture without dominating: these are the qualities of the Ineffable De.

Chapter 11

THE USE OF WHAT IS

Thirty spokes come together at a hole for the axle.

That void makes the wheel useful for a cart.

Baked clay hardens around invisible potential.

That emptiness allows the vessel to hold things.

Doors and windows are cut out of walls.

The openings and gaps make a room roomy.

The use of what is is in what is not.

Chapter 12

BELLIES, NOT EYES

A profusion of colors blinds the eye.

A cacophony of noises deafens the ear.

A flood of flavors numbs the tongue.

Rushing and chasing, the mind becomes unsettled.

Craving and desiring, the heart loses itself on crooked paths.

The Dao-aware satisfy bellies, not eyes.

Chapter 13

FAVOR AND SCORN
ARE BOTH TERRORS

Favor and scorn are both terrors, while bodily harm is to
be prized.

Why are favor and scorn both terrors?

Favor takes power from you. When you don't have it, you
crave it. When you do have it, you dread losing it.

Why should bodily harm be prized?

Calamities are feared only because of the body. If I had no
body, then I would fear no consequences.

Thus, only those who can value the body politic as their
own body should be entrusted with power; only those
who love the body politic as they love themselves deserve
authority.

Chapter 14

THE NATURE OF DAO

Look until you can no longer see; call that dim.

Listen until you can no longer hear; call that faint.

Touch until you can no longer feel; call that minute.

Impossible to trace to the root, these three aspects mingle
into one.

There is no brightness above; neither is there darkness below.

The endless profusion of the unnameable ultimately turns
back to nothingness.

Formless form, image of the unimaginable; call it certain
uncertainty.

Trying to meet it, you'll never see its head.

Trying to follow it, you'll never catch its tail.

Primordial Dao governs all phenomena of the present.

To discern the texture of Dao is to know the source of the
cosmos.

Chapter 15

DON'T SEEK FULFILLMENT

Long ago, the Dao-aware were seen as mysterious and
  insightful, impossible to know.
Because it was impossible to know them, they were inade-
  quately described like this:
Careful, as though fording a river in winter;
Alert, as though surrounded by enemies;
Solemn, like a visiting guest;
Relaxed, like melting ice;
Down-to-earth, like unworked wood;
Open-minded, like an empty valley;
Unaffected, like silt-laden water.
Muddy water, when left alone, gradually clears.
What appears still is merely life in slow motion.
Those keeping to Dao don't seek fulfillment.
Because unfulfilled, the old is also ever-new inside Dao's
  embrace.

Melting Ice

In Wang Anshi's commentary on this chapter, he notes that the *shèngrén* (conventionally translated as "sages") start by merely acting in accordance with Dao but end up becoming one with Dao. In such a state, they see what we cannot see, understand what we don't understand—and we find them mysterious, like a mountain pool whose bottom we cannot fathom.

I suppose it's like when you're climbing a mountain. Only those who have already climbed to the top can see what's on the other side. The way they exclaim and celebrate and marvel and shout—it will all seem mysterious to the rest of us below.

Because we can't quite describe in words what it's like to become one with Dao, we resort to metaphors. One particularly striking image in this chapter is "Relaxed, like melting ice." I find Wang Anshi's gloss on this image especially lovely: "The human spirit begins with no impediments. But it then becomes clouded and knots itself around mundane concerns. The Dao-aware, on the other hand, awaken to dissolve all mundane entanglements, like the melting of ice in spring."

Chapter 16

RETURN TO THE ROOT

Empty your mind to the utmost; be as still as you can.

I observe all things in the cosmos as they emerge, grow, decay, over and over.

All of them ultimately return to the root.

That root is called peace.

To be at peace is to be revitalized.

To be revitalized is the natural condition.

To know the natural condition is to truly understand.

Without knowing the natural condition, one errs into calamity.

Knowing the natural condition, one grows receptive.

Being receptive leads to fairness;

Fairness leads to all-encompassing justice, which is the way of heaven.

The way of heaven is Dao, which is lasting, untroubled even unto death.

Chapter 17

CONCERNING RULERS

The best sort? The people don't even know they're there.
The next-best sort? The people love them and praise them.
A rank below that? The people fear them.
The worst? The people are contemptuous of them.
Because they have no faith, the people do not trust them.

The best rulers are carefree and at ease, for they rarely issue
    orders.
Their task accomplished, the people simply say, "We did it!
    That's the way it should be."

The Ideal Leader

Have you ever worked on a project where there's a shared sense of mission throughout the team, where no one's barking orders but everyone knows what to do, where you felt useful to everyone and everyone felt supportive of you?

Chances are, someone on the team made that happen— not by calling meetings or insisting on a chain of command, not by making big speeches or drawing up detailed schedules, but by getting out of people's way, by dissolving internal entanglements and melting external barriers, by creating space without marking turf, by giving aid without expecting gratitude, by nourishing collaboration without claiming credit. You may be hard-pressed to identify any specific contribution that person made to the project, but without them, the project would have fallen apart.

That's Laozi's idea of leadership.

I think about how we encourage children to develop and express something we call "leadership." I think about how we model and portray and describe and teach what "leadership" is, in fiction and nonfiction, on TV and in games, through hagiographies and TED Talks. I think about how we demand people show "leadership"; how we contrive examples of it in job interviews and on school applications; how we evaluate candidates, perfect strangers with whom we have never worked, for evidence of it.

It's hard not to conclude that we think of leadership as boasting about accomplishments; as speaking up even when you have nothing to say; as making sure your name is as close to the front as possible; as aggression; as pushing; as making demands; as faking; as jostling for power; as getting others to do the work for you; as showing off; as looking good; as credit, territory, anecdotes, certificates; as taking rather than giving.

Meanwhile, the real leaders continue their work in anonymity, like the nourishing presence of water, as they always have done, ensuring that the world will go on and endure.

Zhuangzi tells the following story:

Yang Ziju came to see Laozi.

"Master, let me describe for you a man. He's strong in both body and mind. He's quick, such that there's no question for which he doesn't have a ready answer. His knowledge is both deep and broad: not only does he know a little about everything, but he also possesses keen insights in the areas of his expertise. Even so, he's relentless in his pursuit of more wisdom, never satisfied with himself.

"Would you consider such a person the ideal leader?"

Laozi looked thoughtful, then said, "A person like this is like a skilled clerk, a useful component in the machinery of government. His skills are also his chains; so he's destined to strive and labor, fearful of punishment and craving praise."

"That doesn't sound like a compliment," said Yang Ziju, rather surprised.

"It isn't. A tiger is hunted because it has a beautiful coat. A circus monkey is chained because it's clever and quick. A good tracking hound is leashed because it can catch what others want it to catch. Do you understand now?"

Ziju was silent. At length, he asked, "Master, can you then tell me who would be an ideal leader?"

"An ideal leader's accomplishments would be felt by all under heaven, yet they'd never claim credit for any of it. They nourish and give to everyone, but the people don't become dependent on them. Their efforts are invisible, such that the people can't even come up with a way to praise them; instead, the people celebrate their own skill and honor their own accomplishment."

Chapter 18

DECEIT

When Dao has been abandoned, mercy and justice take its
   place.
When cleverness and wisdom emerge, so does deceit.
Discord in the family leads to talk of familial love, and a
   country teetering on the edge of collapse is filled with
   patriots.

On Benevolence

Some chapters of the *Dao De Jing* seem purposefully directed at those who preach conventional morality. During the era when the book was composed, the most avid lecturers on morality were the Confucians.

As I mentioned earlier, there are many stories of meetings between Confucius and Laozi. Zhuangzi, the Daoist master, tells several.

In these stories, Confucius, the founder of Confucianism, always comes humbly to Laozi and asks Laozi about Dao. The two then have a conversation in which the differences between Confucianism and Daoism are starkly displayed, and the personalities of the two great teachers vividly contrasted.

Now, it bears remembering that Zhuangzi's stories have an agenda. Sima Qian, the Grand Historian, describes Zhuangzi like this:

His intellect was so wide-ranging that there seemed no subject that he didn't know, though the core of his philosophy was based on the teachings of Laozi. His compositions total more than ten thousand words, with the parable being his favorite literary form. Some of his works, such as "The Fisherman," "The Robber Named Zhi," and "Breaking Chests," were intended to mock Confucians and spread Laozi's philosophy. The people named in his stories should be understood as fictional characters, not real individuals. As a writer, Zhuangzi was exceptionally skilled at using colorful metaphors and analogies to ridicule Confucianism and Mohism. Even the most prominent masters of learning of his day could not escape his barbs. He wrote only to please himself, refusing to temper his words for any reason. As a result, he was never valued by those in power.

The best way to understand Zhuangzi's stories is to treat them similarly to how we treat Plato's dialogues. The situations and quotes may be fictional, but the fiction reveals a deeper truth.

Let's begin with a meeting between Confucius and Laozi, as imagined by Zhuangzi:

Confucius, the great teacher, spent much of his life roaming among the constantly warring petty states, trying to persuade them to adopt his philosophy of benevolence.

One day, he thought of bringing some books to the court of Zhou in the west for safekeeping and teaching.

Zilu, one of Confucius's favorite disciples, said, "Master, I heard that Laozi, an archive keeper at the court of Zhou, has retired and returned to his home. Why don't you go talk with him to get some advice on which books to bring to the court?"

Confucius thought this was an excellent idea, and so they went.

Once they got to Laozi's home, Confucius began to explain which books he thought would be good. But Laozi said nothing, neither approving nor disapproving. Alarmed, Confucius redoubled his efforts, unfolding books and pointing to specific passages to support his arguments. Soon, Laozi's floor was covered in character-laden bamboo strips, making it hard to even get up and walk.

Laozi broke in, "I'm drowning in your words here. Can you summarize for me the key points of these books you prize so much?"

"The key of all these books," said Confucius, "is benevolence."

"Ah. Then . . . is benevolence part of human nature?"

"Certainly. Without benevolence, how can people of virtue establish their good name? Without benevolence, how can society be secure? Benevolence must be part of human nature, for without it nothing can be done."

Laozi thought this over. "Can you then enlighten me on what is benevolence?"

Pleased to be able to lecture on his core teaching, Confucius intoned, "To have a just heart in harmony with all creation; to love everyone without selfish preference—these are the conditions for benevolence."

"Ha." Laozi shook his head. "A lot of pretty words meaning nothing. 'To love everyone' is the same as loving no one. And to be 'without selfish preference' is the most selfish preference of all—you want everyone to praise you for your superiority."

"But-but-but—"

Laozi didn't give Confucius a chance to spout any more of his theories. "Your goal, to have everyone be able to take care of their own needs, is good. But observe: heaven and earth have their eternal patterns; the sun and the moon shine with their own light; the stars hold their own places; the beasts and birds gather in their own herds and flocks; and the trees and shrubs live their own cycles and need no one's help to remain upright.

"Master Confucius, you should simply let human nature express itself and follow the path inherent in the cosmos. Then what you desire will accomplish itself. Why do you strain all your energy to hold up the banner of 'benevolence,' which is akin to striking a bell to find a fugitive—the louder you ring, the farther they run. You're merely making it harder for people to know the right thing to do."

Chapter 19

PLAIN SILK AND UNWORKED WOOD

Abandon reverence and calculation, and the people will
benefit a hundredfold.
Cease talk of mercy and justice, and the people will reclaim
kindness and goodwill.
Eliminate profit and design, and there will be no more robbers and thieves.
To frame the law by these three rules is still insufficient.
Follow this principle: be like plain silk and unworked wood,
undyed by desire and speculation, unadorned with learning and worry.

Mercy and Justice

Abstract terms like *love* and *goodwill* are among the most difficult words to translate between languages. The causes for this are many. For one thing, abstract terms draw arbitrary borders around related concepts that blend and merge into one another, and different languages draw such borders differently. (Consider, for example, C. S. Lewis's famous parsing of *love* into four related concepts separately named in Greek.) For another, abstractions gain meaning via concrete applications. That is why *liberty*, transmuted by Patrick Henry's "Give me liberty or give me death!" will occupy a different semantic space from Chinese *xiāoyáo*, coined by Zhuangzi to express that highest state of absolute liberty of the spirit for the Dao-aware, like the flight of a mythical bird soaring far above the sublunary sphere.

Thus, in translation, for abstractions there is always slippage between the source language and the target language. When a word such as the Chinese *xǐhuan* is translated as the English *like*, much is lost, for *xǐhuan* can also mean love in the romantic sense, fondness, enjoyment, delight, and many other related concepts. But at the same time, much is also added, for the English *like* contains within it multitudes that are not encompassed by the Chinese *xǐhuan*. The two words do not function like the docking ports of two spacecraft, seamlessly mapping one to the other. Rather, they're like two trees that serve similar purposes for their respective communities: marking the entrance to the village for weary travelers, sheltering songbirds and nut-hoarding rodents from the rain, concealing lovers meeting by the moon, shading laborers from the blazing sun. Yet, having been shaped by distinct climates, geographies, genes, and histories, the two trees have branched and ramified into two different filigreed designs. When these two forms are brought together, the rough shape of one may remind us of the rough shape of the other, but the differences are at least as great as the regions of overlap. To understand fully where one word can substitute for another and where it cannot requires not just dictionaries, literatures, histories, but two lifetimes of experience.

(While any translation requires embracing slippages that both lose and gain, subtract and add, I've left *Dao* and *De* largely untranslated throughout my rendition of the *Dao De Jing*. These words are simply too important, too *plain*, to bear artful attempts to carve them to fit the shapes of existing English words. While it's possible to translate *Dao* as "the way" and *De* as "virtue" (or "power," if one goes by etymology) in some cases, the slippage, in general, is too great and requires the English words to be given entirely new meanings. It's preferable to retain the Chinese words and import them into English.)

The words *rén* (仁) and *yì* (義) are among those abstract trees in the Chinese semantic forest that have no exact correspondence in English. Emphasized by Confucius (and Mencius, who expanded on Confucius's teachings), these words, jointly and separately, are among the most important in Confucianism. Variously translated as "benevolence and justice" or "morality and ethics" or "generosity and righteousness" or "compassionate love and justified duty"—and many other pairs—the words mean all of these and none of these.

I ended up picking "mercy and justice" largely because I was trained as a lawyer and because I love Portia's speech from *The Merchant of Venice*: "In the course of justice, none of us should see salvation: we do pray for mercy." I'd like to think that Laozi and Confucius would approve. Heaven and earth neither impose justice nor dole out mercy—but we can't help but yearn for both.

Laozi's words, if rendered literally into English (though as I've just explained, this is not possible), would mean something like "end mercy, abandon justice," a rather striking dismissal of the foundational concepts of Confucianism.

The Guodian manuscripts do not contain this admonition at all. Instead, the manuscripts speak of ending fraud and abandoning hypocrisy. Based on this, some have argued that the received text contains deliberate edits made by later scribes, either by radical Daoists to emphasize the attack on Confucianism (which Zhuangzi and his students were known for) or by Confucians intent on making Laozi look bad.

As I prefer to focus on the beast rather than the tracks left behind, I don't think it matters much either way. Elsewhere in the *Dao De Jing*, Laozi notes, "When Dao has been abandoned, mercy and justice take its place." I take "end mercy, abandon justice" to mean that *talk* of these concepts, arguments over what they mean and don't mean, clever ways to twist the words to cover anything and nothing at all, is pointless and counterproductive. Abstractions are like mannequins, capable of modeling any outfit you please. It is not the words, but something both smaller and grander than the words that matters. It's about concrete gestures of kindness to our fellow humans as well as the willingness to abide by the movements of the unceasing bellows between sky and earth; it's about taking pleasure in a crooked tree or a chipped bowl as well as lamenting the deaths of soldiers who fight for our enemies; it's about the mercy that manifests by seeking the greatest freedom for the individual soul as well as the justice in accepting that heaven and earth neither love nor hate us.

Chapter 20

THE MILK OF DAO

How much does a plea differ from an order?

How short is the distance between good and ill?

Impossible not to fear what everyone says to fear; such it
has always been since the beginning of time.

The multitudes throng in excitement, a celebratory banquet,
a spring outing.

I stand in serene solitude, unmoved: carefree, like a baby
before it could laugh; unmoved, since there's no place
where I must be.

They have more than they need; I less than my fill.

I have a fool's heart, carefree!

They shine and sparkle, I stay dull and obscure.

They parse and examine, I remain simple and silent.

Unremarkable, like the ocean, and likewise boundless,
beyond sight.

They have their talents and purposes, I my clumsy useless-
ness.

Unlike them, I'm sustained by Dao, the one and only mother's
milk.

Ideophones

Laozi fills this chapter with ideophones, which are common in Chinese, but not nearly as prevalent in English.

Ideophones are words that, through their phonetic properties, evoke the *feeling* of an abstract concept. English examples would include words like *knickknack* and *helter-skelter*. The phonetic patterns in these words hint at the triviality, confusion, messiness, in the *ideas*. (They are related to, but different from, onomatopoeias, which are words that imitate sounds. Ideophones generally don't imitate sounds so much as re-create *feelings* through sounds—they are a form of synesthesia for the rest of us.)

Laozi doesn't just use existing ideophones. He creates them anew here, often by doubling a word, almost like the way toddlers who are learning to speak would double syllables or words to emphasize, intensify, suggest, something *more* than the word itself.

An example may make this clearer. I'll give a transliteration of the line in pinyin first, followed by the translation.

沌沌兮，如嬰兒之未孩；儽儽兮，若無所歸。

Dùndùn xī, rú yīngér zhī wèi hái; lěilěi xī, ruò wú suǒ guī.

Carefree, like a baby before it could laugh; unmoved, since there's no place where I must be.

In the first half of the line, *dùn* (沌) by itself means "chaos" or "confusion." Doubled, *dùndùn* suggests the prelinguistic state of cognition, when sense isn't yet distinct from sensation, when syllable hasn't yet emerged from sound—the mental state of a newborn. I chose to render it as "carefree."

In the second half of the line, *lěi* (儽) by itself is an adjective describing someone dejected, spiritless, at a loss. Doubled, *lěilěi* piles exhaustion upon loss upon dejection upon listlessness, describing someone who has nowhere to return to, utterly lost—paradoxically also the state of someone at one with Dao and therefore feeling no pressure to be anywhere. I chose to make the implied reversal in meaning explicit in the translation.

Xīxī, dùndùn, lěilěi, zhāozhāo, hūnhūn, mènmèn—the ideophones make for a powerful literary technique that induces the reader's mind to fall into their hypnotic and meditative rhythm, since the ideal state of mind for Laozi is literally to be "like a baby before it could laugh or babble."

The effect is untranslatable, for such a linguistic mechanism is not generalizable to contemporary English. But perhaps in our minds we can all try to slow down and repeat the words, doubling them hypnotically, trying to be as much like a newborn as possible.

Chapter 21

THE FORM BEFORE FORMS

The greatest De, the life we're meant to live, can only follow
    from the flow of Dao.
Dao isn't fixed, circumscribed, certain.
Unformed, it has form.
Insubstantial, it has substance.
Macroscopic and microscopic, it has an essence.
That essence is the truth, worthy of trust.
From time immemorial, its name has persisted, the name by
    which the source of all may be known.
How can I know the form before all forms? Through Dao.

Chapter 22

BY BENDING, THE WHOLE FITS

By flexing, the whole fits;

By bending, the rod remains unbroken.

That which dips fills;

That which is withered cannot decay.

Having few means having all; having much ends in confusion.

The Dao-aware hold to one path:

Without showing off, all is clearly seen;

Without presumption, right reveals itself from wrong;

Without self-praise, honor gathers to them;

Without self-regard, their legacy endures.

Because they don't strive against others, no one strives
  against them.

"By bending, the whole fits." This is no empty advice, but
  the original truth.

Chapter 23

NATURE SPEAKS LITTLE

Nature speaks little.

A violent gale subsides after a few hours;

A pelting shower clears before the end of the day.

Who's responsible for the wind and the rain? Heaven and
earth.

Heaven and earth don't go on and on. Why should people?

Act in harmony with Dao, and you are one with Dao;

Act in harmony with De, and you are one with De;

Act at a loss, and you are lost.

When you are one with Dao, Dao is happy to have you;

When you are one with De, De is happy to have you;

When you are at a loss, the lost are happy to have you.

The faithless will be trusted by no one.

Chapter 24

ON TIPTOES

You can't stand for long on tiptoes;
Nor can you walk far by leaping every step.
Those who show off will be forgotten;
Those who presume will learn nothing;
Those who praise themselves will be without honor;
Those who think much of themselves will not endure.
Dao thinks of these as rotten food, misshapen tumors,
Disgusting things best avoided by the Dao-aware.

Chapter 25

WHAT IS DAO?

Something from primordial chaos, there before heaven or
  earth.
Soundless, formless, complete unto itself, circulating without
  cease, perhaps the progenitor of the cosmos.
Lacking a better name, I call it Dao.
Lacking a better description, I call it Grand.
Grand: passing and flowing.
Flowing: broad and distant.
Distant: returning to home.
Dao, heaven, and earth are all grand, as is humankind.
The cosmos has four grand aspects, and we are one of them.
The humane derives from the earthly, which is derived from
  the heavenly, which is derived from Dao.
Dao is the pattern of nature.

Chapter 26

THE ROOT OF LIGHTNESS

The root of lightness is weight;

The master of recklessness is repose.

The Dao-aware will not abandon the baggage cart after a
    long day's journey.

Even when surrounded by luxuries and exotic sights, they
    hold still like a swallow at ease.

Why does a lord of ten thousand chariots treat the fate of
    the world so lightly?

Flightiness is without root;

Aimless churning has no master.

I Would Rather Drag My Tail through the Mud

I love the image of the Dao-aware swallow sitting at ease in a muddy nest, unmoved by the lure of exotic sights and luxuries all around. When you hold to Dao and Dao anchors you, there is no more fear of loss, no more craving for favor, no more terror of the vicissitudes of the mortal cosmos. The mind stills; the trembling in the limbs ceases. You can accept the dance of terror and beauty that goes on forever between heaven and earth, in spite of you and also because of you.

That is the ultimate state of freedom, *xiāoyáo*, both freedom *from* and freedom *to*. Too little has been said about the Daoist focus on freedom, a concept that we in the West all too often act as if had been invented by us.

Not that most of us can attain that state of true freedom most of the time, or even anytime.

I'm reminded of another Dao-aware creature who lives close to mud and is rooted by the weight of its own baggage cart. Zhuangzi tells the following story:

One day, Zhuangzi was sitting on the bank of the Pu River when two ministers of the king of Chu approached him.

"Master," they said, "our king has heard reports of your talent and virtue. He would like you to serve him and become his valued servant. He'll entrust the administration of his powerful state to you so that you can realize your political ideals and ambitions. Come, let's go at once."

Zhuangzi held on to his fishing pole, not even sparing the two ministers a glance.

"What is this?" The two ministers were amazed. "Do you not understand what an incredible opportunity you've been given?"

"I heard a story," said Zhuangzi, "that there was once a turtle possessing great magic in the state of Chu. It died three thousand years ago. But even now, the king wraps its shell in silk and stores the bundle in a bamboo ceremonial vessel, keeping the treasured carapace in the holiest chamber of the state temple."

The two ministers looked at each other, unsure where Zhuangzi was going with this.

"Tell me," Zhuangzi said, "do you think the turtle would have preferred to die so that its hollow shell could be honored afterward, or to live so that it could drag its tail through the mud?"

"To . . . live," the two ministers said.

"That's right. You have your answer. Tell the king that I would rather drag my tail through the mud."

Chapter 27

A GOOD KNOT HAS NO ROPE

A skilled hiker leaves no track.

An adept speaker leaves no flaw.

A good accountant uses no counting sticks.

A good door has no bolt but can't be opened.

A good knot has no rope but can't be untied.

The Dao-aware save everyone without leaving anyone, preserve all things without abandoning anything.

This is a hidden light.

Good people can be teachers for those not so good.

And the not-so-good people can be examples for the good.

Without honoring teachers or valuing examples, even the clever would be mired in great confusion.

This is a crucial mystery.

Chapter 28

WHAT IS DE?

Knowing male but holding to female, be like the world's
river channel.

To be the world's river channel is to keep eternal De, to return
to the state of a newborn.

Knowing brightness but holding to darkness, be the world's
example.

To be the world's example is to not err from eternal De, to
return to the unbounded.

Knowing honor, but holding to disgrace, be the world's
gorge.

To be the world's gorge is to be filled with eternal De, to
return to primitive simplicity.

Simplicity has endless uses. With it, the Dao-aware become
great leaders, their grand design seamless because it is
uncut.

Chapter 29

THE GRASPING WILL LOSE

Those who wish to take the world by doing I think are destined to fail.

The world is a sacred thing, unobtainable by doing, impossible to seize by force.

The doing will fail; the grasping will lose.

The Dao-aware will not do, and thus they won't fail nor lose.

Among people, some are rushers, and some are followers;

Some stroll and exhale calmly, and some run and pant;

Some are strong, and some are weak;

Some prefer the sure thing, and some love risk.

That's why the Dao-aware eliminate what is too much, too rich, too extreme.

Chapter 30

VICTORY

When you follow Dao to help rulers, don't try to dominate
the world with an army.

Force invites more force.

Wherever an army marches, brambles spring up.

Whenever an army conquers, famine comes next.

Stop as soon as the objective has been achieved; don't let
victory push you to seek more.

After victory, don't swagger, boast, swell with pride.

Victory because there's no other choice, not to feed strength.

From a peak of strength there's nowhere to go but down.

Whoever doesn't follow Dao will come to an early end.

Chapter 31

ARMS ARE SINISTER THINGS

Arms are sinister things, despised, and the Dao-aware don't
    tolerate them.

At peace, we prize the left.

At war, we prize the right.

The wise don't rely on weapons.

Even when turning to them as a last resort, it's best to treat
    them with indifference.

Delight not in victory, for to delight in victory is to delight
    also in killing.

Pleasure in killing will never win over the world.

When speaking of pleasant deeds, we prefer the left;

For unpleasant deeds, we prefer the right.

The lieutenant stands on the left;

The commander stands on the right.

From this, we know to treat acts of war as burial rites, to be
    attended only with heavy hearts.

The murdered multitudes deserve tearful mourning;

Victories ought to be seen as funerals.

Laozi's Death

In this chapter, Laozi speaks about death and death dealing, which spin the eternal wheel of suffering that we seem unable to escape from. When reading it, I'm reminded of the following story from Zhuangzi, concerning Laozi's own death:

After Laozi died, his friend Qin Shi went to his wake.

Qin Shi let out a few quiet sobs in front of the body, turned around, and left.

Laozi's students ran after him.

"I thought you are my teacher's friend!" one of the disciples shouted.

"I am."

"Then why are you acting so cold?" The disciple's voice shook with barely suppressed rage.

"You misunderstand me. At first I would have agreed with you that it's only human to mourn my friend and cry. But when I went inside, I saw elders sobbing as though they had lost a son; I saw young people bawling as though they had lost their mother."

The disciples nodded. They thought those people were demonstrating the right way to mourn their master.

"But Laozi wasn't their son or their mother," said Qin Shi. "Do you think it's possible that some of them were expressing sentiments that they didn't really feel, squeezing out tears that they didn't need to shed?"

The disciples looked at one another, unable to respond.

Qin She went on, "To cry because you're expected to cry; to say things because convention demands that you say them—that is going against the pattern of nature and submitting to the tyranny of false sentiment. Laozi came into the world because it was his time; likewise, he departed because he followed the flow of Dao. Confident in his submission to Dao, neither our laughter nor our tears will bother him. The ancients would say that he has been released by the heavens."

Candles and torches may burn out, but fire will always glow brightly, generation after generation.

I think about the contrast between what Laozi says concerning how we should think of those killed in wars and what Zhuangzi says concerning how we should remember those we love who have passed on.

The murdered multitudes deserve tearful mourning;
Victories ought to be seen as funerals.
Confident in his submission to Dao, neither our laughter nor
    our tears will bother him. The ancients would say that
    he has been released by the heavens.

Laozi and Zhuangzi both emphasize sincerity of emotion, the primacy of how it *feels* over how it *looks*, but like the eternal dance of beauty and terror, two aspects of the same Providence, there is a grand mystery here in the pair of contrasting sentiments. Heaven and earth may shed no tears for the dead, for to them we're all straw dogs. But we should mourn all those who die in wars, friend and foe, coward and hero, the faithless and the trustworthy. We should also smile at the departure of our loved ones and say, "They've merged into the flux of Dao, like swallows in muddy nests, like turtles dragging tails through the mud, like plain silk and unworked wood, lasting because they've stopped seeking."

Chapter 32

THE FLOW OF DAO

Dao is always unnamed and unworked.

Though small, it will submit to nothing else in the cosmos.

Lords aware of it will have everyone as willing subjects.

Heaven and earth, in harmony with Dao, yield honey and dew,
  and the people, unordered, will share in the commonweal.

To regulate the world, we invent names, ranks, positions.

But the naming cannot go too far, lest it err into danger.

The flow of Dao in the cosmos is like the commingling of all
  streams in the ocean.

Chapter 33

WINNING AGAINST YOURSELF

Knowing others is cleverness, but knowing yourself is wisdom.

Winning against others requires force, but winning against
yourself requires strength.

The content are wealthy.

The constant are beyond ambition.

Holding to your place is how you endure.

True longevity is to die without perishing.

Chapter 34

SMALL AND GRAND

Grand Dao swells like the tide, reaching this way and that.

All things in the cosmos are sustained by it, though it says
   nothing of what it does.

The work done, it lays no claim.

To clothe and maintain all things without claiming to be
   their master is why we say it is small.

To have the attachment of all things without dominating
   them is why we say it is grand.

It is great because it never considers itself to be so.

The Bird Named Peng
and the Fish Named Kun

In the far northern ocean there is a giant fish named kun. It is so large that its body stretches for thousands of miles. Sometimes it turns into a bird, which we call peng. The wingspan of the peng is also thousands of miles. When it takes to the air with a great effort, its wings hang down like clouds draping from the heavens. Effortlessly, this sky-veiling bird soars across the world, winging its way to the antipodean southern ocean.

According to ancient books recording strange tales of travelers to distant realms, the peng takes six months to make this journey, never landing once. The typhoons that terrorize all other creatures don't bother the peng at all, for the bird views them as mere updrafts that provide lift, helping it to rise as high as ninety thousand miles, near the starry empyrean.

Now, as the peng glides overhead, the shadow it casts is so terrifying that cicadas and turtledoves cease their songs and dive for cover. Only long after the giant bird has passed do the little creatures emerge from tangled clumps of grass and holes in trees.

"What a silly creature!" they mock and jeer. "When we take off, the farthest we can get to is the top of that scholar-tree or the tip of that sloping roof. Sometimes we don't even bother with that because there are plenty of worms and discarded grain on the ground for us to eat. Why would you ever want to fly ninety thousand miles up? Fool! Idiot!"

Only the deep ocean can carry grand ships. But if you pour a cup of water on the floor, even bits of grass and chaff can float upon it with ease.

There are mushrooms that live an entire life in one morning, never knowing the crimson glow of a sunset or the cold light of the stars. The summer cicada chirps throughout its life, but it's dead by fall and never has to contend with winter or celebrate spring. In the far south there is a tree called mingling, which treats the passage of five hundred years as merely one season. And then there's the dachun tree of ancient times, which added a single growth ring every eight thousand years. Compared to these, what is even the longest human span?

The world contains both the grand and the small, and one can barely understand the other.

Think of those clever people who manage to obtain competitive government posts, whose conduct is praised by their constituents, whose competence and vision are satisfactory to grand lords, and whose judgment is trusted by a nation—they probably view themselves with great satisfaction. But how are they different from the turtledoves and cicadas who laugh at the freedom of the peng soaring overhead?

The Dao-aware don't have selves; they don't have accomplishments; they don't have honor, reputation, name.

This is one of my all-time favorite stories from Zhuangzi. Some have read into this tale a human hierarchy. They think it's better to be the peng bird than the cicadas and turtledoves. They think it's better to soar high above, to move heaven and earth, to call forth storms and make waves, to rule, to dominate, to be a giant form skidding across the world, casting a shadow upon those below, to frighten, to shock and awe.

But this is a total misreading. The *xiāoyáo* peng is grand because it's free; it's free because it's beyond ambition.

Chapter 35

TASTY FOOD AND PLEASANT MUSIC

The image of Dao draws the hearts of all.

They come to it, unguarded, at peace.

Tasty food and pleasant music make all passersby stop,

But a description of Dao sounds plain, devoid of flavor,

For Dao is impossible to see, impossible to hear,

Though its power is limitless in use.

Chapter 36

TO BE TAKEN, IT MUST FIRST BE GIVEN

To be gathered, it must first be scattered.

To be weakened, it must first be strengthened.

To be demolished, it must first be erected.

To be taken, it must first be given.

This is both subtle and obvious.

The soft and weak triumph over the hard and strong.

Fish cannot live apart from deep water.

The state doesn't brandish its sharp tools.

Machiavellian

The state doesn't brandish its sharp tools.

Many have read into the final line of this verse a Machiavellian sentiment. Sometimes, the line is even rendered as "The state doesn't brandish its weapons to the people."

Is Laozi advising rulers to pretend not to have a monopoly on force, to conceal its essential oppressive function, in order to deceive the people into compliance?

Some have argued that this is a later addition by some copyist, perhaps an attempt to make Daoism relevant for those in power.

Although Laozi and Zhuangzi both explicitly address sections of their books to rulers, Daoism has proven to be essentially incompatible with governments. At its heart, Daoism insists that those with power over others give it up; good luck trying to convince anyone with power—in any form of government—to willingly do so.

Historically, the authorities have either tried to make Daoism irrelevant by portraying it as the philosophy of losers and malcontents, or to co-opt it by twisting Laozi's words into "practical advice" for exercising power in subtle and devious ways. (Sima Qian's attempt to link Daoists with Legalists seems to me to be the result of this school of thinking.)

Even today, the bookshelves are replete with business and self-help books that proclaim to unlock the secrets of Laozi and Zhuangzi to help you win friends and influence people, to make money without much work, to triumph in office politics without appearing to plot and contend.

But Laozi's book has always resisted such attempts. Like water, it slips through the fingers of those who would try to grasp it and make it serve power.

In any event, I've kept this possible later addition to Laozi's text because I like Wang Anshi's interpretation of it. He identifies the state with the Dao-aware, then writes, "Like fish who cannot leave their pool, the sharp tools of the Dao-aware are hidden within the small and subtle, inseparable from unworked nature."

As the *Dao De Jing* notes in another chapter, the Dao-aware should be

Keen but don't cut

and

Bright but don't dazzle.

A keenness is necessary to pierce through the nonsense we've layered around ourselves. But the keenness is nourishing rather than harmful, yielding rather than aggressive. It's incapable of being brandished.

95

Chapter 37

EVER DOING NOTHING

Dao is ever doing nothing so that nothing is undone.
If those with power can hold to its path, then all things will
     take care of themselves.
When things take care of themselves, desires spring forth.
I would then enfold desires with nameless simplicity, until
     desires are quieted, and all is tranquility.

PART II

THE BOOK
OF DE

Chapter 38

THE VIRTUE OF DE

Those with High De don't flaunt their virtue, for they have true De.

Those with Low De don't deviate from virtue, for they don't have true De.

The former don't do and don't think much of doing.

The latter don't do but think they got much done.

The benevolent do but don't think much of themselves.

The righteous do and think often of their deeds.

The punctilious *would* do, and when no one responds, they raise their arms and drag others with them.

That is why those who have lost the way of Dao resort to the virtue of De;

Those who have lost De resort to benevolence;

Those who have lost benevolence resort to righteousness;

Those who have lost righteousness resort to propriety.

Codes are born from the thinning of trust, the beginning of chaos.

Prophets only fancy they know Dao; they're in fact the beginning of foolishness.

Grand souls prefer the concrete to the thin, the substantial to the fanciful.

Chapter 39

JADE AND STONE

What do they become when at one with Dao?

Heaven, clear;

Earth, tranquil;

Spirits, animated;

Gorges, filled;

Grand lords with power, real leaders;

All things, alive.

On the other hand, when apart from Dao:

Heaven loses clarity, threatening to crack;

Earth loses tranquility, threatening to quake;

Spirits lose vitality, threatening to fade;

Gorges are drained, threatening drought.

Grand lords lose their virtue, threatening to fall;

All things lose sustenance, threatening extinction.

That is why the foundation of the noble is base, and the high
is built on the low.

Sovereigns call themselves alone, bereft, unsupported—isn't
it because they know they come from the base and low?

Thus seek not to be praised like jade for its bright glow, but
to be as durable as plain stone.

Chapter 40

WHAT IS NOT

Opposition is the movement of Dao.

Weakness is the use of Dao.

All things in the cosmos come from what is.

But what is comes from what is not.

Chapter 41

IF IT'S NOT LAUGHED AT

Some hear about Dao and strive to practice it;
Some hear about Dao and vacillate around it;
Some hear about Dao and laugh at it.
If it's not laughed at, it isn't worthy of being Dao.
Thus, ancient wisdom tells us that the bright path of Dao
    appears obscure;
The advancing Dao appears to retreat;
The straight Dao appears twisted.
The highest De appears as a low gully;
The broadest De appears not enough;
The upstanding De appears lazy;
The pure and true appears cloudy;
The clearest also appears disdained;
The great square contains no corners;
The great vessel is unworked;
The grand music has little sound;
The grand shape has no form;
Dao is hidden, having no name.
It gives to all and by it all is sustained.

Late or Unworked?

The great square contains no corners;
The great vessel is unworked;
The grand music has little sound;
The grand shape has no form;

Here's another example where I've adopted the Mawang-dui version of the *Dao De Jing* in preference to the received text.

In the received text, the second line is rendered "The great vessel is finished late." The line has entered the Chinese language as a fixed expression to describe that those who would accomplish much may take a long time to acquire their skills and opportunities.

In context, it seems to me clear that "the great vessel is unworked," as written in one of the Mawangdui manuscripts, is much more in line with the rest of the verse. Each line is composed as a pair of opposites, like the yin-yang fish. Moreover, the image of unworked wood, pervasive in the rest of the book, fits perfectly here.

Chapter 42

HOLD YANG AND BEAR YIN

Dao gives birth to the one;

The one gives birth to the pair;

The pair gives birth to the three;

The three give birth to all things.

All things hold yang and bear yin and in their contention find harmony.

People fear to be alone, bereft, unsupported, yet the grand lords call themselves by those terms.

Thus, in all things, sometimes the harm benefits, and sometimes the benefit harms.

What others have said, I also teach:

Those who live by the sword die in pieces; that is the foundation of my teaching.

Chapter 43

NO PRESENCE, NO SEAMS

The softest thing in the cosmos has free rein through the
hardest.
That which has no presence penetrates that which has no
seams.
That is how I know the power of doing by not doing, teaching
by not speaking.
There's nothing comparable in the universe.

Chapter 44

WHICH IS MORE PRECIOUS?

Which is more dear, your fame or your life?

Which is more precious, your body or your fortune?

Which is the worse disease, to profit or to lose?

The more you desire, the more it costs.

The more you hoard, the more you'll waste.

To be content with what you have is to never be disgraced,

And to know when to stop is how you avoid catastrophe.

This is the only way to endure.

Chapter 45

PERFECTLY FLAWED

The most perfected appears flawed, but it will never be
exhausted.
The most fulfilled appears to be hollow, but it will never be
emptied out.
The straightest path appears full of twists and turns.
The highest craft appears unworked.
The best orator sounds plain.
The still wins over the restless; the cool over the impetuous.
Serenity governs the cosmos.

Chapter 46

CONTENTMENT

Warhorses plow fields when Dao flows unimpeded.

Mares deliver foals on the battlefield when Dao is lost.

There's no greater disaster than dissatisfaction, no greater
fault than to crave more than you have.

The contentment of being content lasts evermore.

Chapter 47

THE FARTHER SOME GO

To know what happens in the cosmos doesn't require step-
ping outside the door.
To understand the ways of heaven doesn't require looking
outside the window.
The farther some go, the less they know.
The Dao-aware know without trekking, understand without
seeing, finish without doing.

Gaining Wisdom

At the heart of Daoism is the idea that only the fool has true wisdom. Striving to be learned, to study, to analyze and calculate and assess and plot . . . moves you away from wisdom. The Dao-aware don't seek to "enlighten" others; wisdom comes from within. This idea almost invites misunderstanding and misapplication—again, words mislead.

Here's a story from Zhuangzi on the difficulties of "learning" wisdom:

Confucius, despondent, came to see Laozi and said, "I've studied the ancient books for such a long time and know them forward and backward. I can recite for you every detail of the laws and rituals of past golden ages. I've composed comprehensive treatises on how rulers who deviate from the wisdom of ancient philosopher-kings are sure to fall into ruin, drawing on seventy-two such foolish princes as examples. Yet, not a single grand lord in the world has followed my ideals. Why is it so difficult? Is it because it's too hard to persuade people through reason? Or is it because the right path, the one and only Dao, is so resistant to being illuminated?"

"It's a good thing that you didn't run into someone who would actually be capable of reforming and remaking the world according to your vision!" said Laozi. "Those classics that you mention . . . they're nothing more than old trails walked by ancient princes, not the animated minds that left those trails. All these things you mention are just tracks, tracks left by roaming feet. But are dead tracks the same as living feet?

"Look about you: The birds and beasts carry on with their lives following patterns only they know, heeding the call of their diverse natures. Nature cannot be altered; fate cannot be thwarted; time cannot be stopped; and Dao cannot be blocked. When you are aware of Dao, there's nowhere you cannot go. But when you aren't aware of Dao, there's no place where you'll be free."

Confucius left to be by himself for three months. When he returned to see Laozi, he looked both more and less confused.

"Crows and magpies hatch from eggs in nests," Confucius said. "Young fish come out of frothy bubbles. The bees and wasps emerge from airy nothingness. And for us, born from the womb, we cry for the loss of each moment even as we live through it. For so long I've not paid attention to the flow of ceaseless change in everything around me. But unless I become one with ceaseless change, how can I seek to change anyone?"

"I congratulate you," said Laozi. "For you're starting to be aware."

Chapter 48

MORE AND LESS

Each day of studying the world leads you to *more*.
Each day of harmonizing with Dao inclines you to *less*.
Less, still less, until you do nothing.
Do nothing so that nothing is undone.
To take the world lastingly requires a mind empty of deeds.
A mind yearning for deeds, on the other hand, can never
 take the world.

Chapter 49

KIND TO THE UNKIND

The Dao-aware hold no heart of their own, but treat the
hearts of the people as theirs.

I'm kind to those who are kind, but also to the unkind;

In the end, kindness holds.

I'm trusting to those who are trusting, but also to the
untrusting;

In the end, trust holds.

For the world, breath by breath, the Dao-aware stir their
hearts into clouded simplicity.

The people focus on what can be seen and heard; the Dao-
aware have returned all to the wholeness of the newborn
baby.

Chapter 50

THE REALM OF DEATH

On the journey from birth to death,

Out of ten people,

Three live long lives,

Three die early,

And three more, who could have lived long lives, die early

    because they put themselves in death's realm.

Why?

Because they craved to live too much.

It is said that the wise can trek without encountering rhinos

    and tigers,

And can be drafted without worrying about arms.

For them, rhinos have nowhere to thrust their horns;

Tigers have nowhere to swipe their claws;

Soldiers have nowhere to slash their swords.

Why?

Because the wise don't enter the realm of death.

Chapter 51

DAO'S HONOR, DE'S VALUE

Dao births; De nourishes.

Things take their forms; patterns propel them forward.

That's why all things in the cosmos honor Dao and value De.

How does Dao get its honor? How does De get its value?

By not reordering the order of nature.

So Dao births; De nourishes.

Generates, rears, shelters, heals, cares, protects.

To create without possessing, to give without expecting, to
nurture without dominating: these are the qualities of
Ineffable De.

Chapter 52

CLARITY AND STRENGTH

The origin of heaven and earth is also the mother of all.

Knowing the mother, it's possible to know all her children.

Knowing all the children, and still holding to the way of the
mother, no catastrophe can befall.

Block off the mind's windows, seal up its doors, and you
need not labor the rest of your life.

But tear the mind open, flood it with worldly confusion,
there will be no salvation for you.

To see the minuscule is what we call "clarity."

To hold to the yielding is what we call "strength."

Use the light to reilluminate the source;

Carry yourself away from danger and inherit the eternal.

Chapter 53

DAO IS WIDE AND STRAIGHT

Let me know but a little, as I stride down Dao's grand road,
  I fear straying.
Though Dao is wide and straight, people love shortcuts.
The palaces are magnificent, the fields deserted, the ware-
  houses empty.
Lords stride about in glorious clothes, carry sharp swords,
  eat so much good food that they're sick of it, and hoard
  wealth beyond measure.
They're bandits and robbers, having wandered far from Dao.

Chapter 54

EXPANDING DE

Well-built things won't be uprooted;

Well-held things won't be cast off.

Thus the offerings continue without cease, generation after
   generation.

Applying these principles to the self, De is true;

To the family, De is abundant;

To the town, De is honored;

To the nation, De is thriving;

To the world, De is universal;

So it is to perceive the self with the self,

To perceive the family with the family,

To perceive the town with the town,

To perceive the nation with the nation,

To perceive the world with the world.

How do I know the world then? Just like that.

Chapter 55

THE DE OF BABIES

Someone who holds the power of De is like a newborn baby.

Venomous insects don't sting them;

Fierce beasts don't seize them;

Swooping raptors don't claw them.

Their bones and sinews are weak, yet their grasp is strong.

They know not the union of male and female, yet their organ
   is erect,

For they're filled with the essence of vitality,

They cry all day without their voice cracking,

For they're at the peak of harmony.

To know harmony is to know the eternal.

To know the eternal is to achieve clarity.

Boosting life leads to foreboding uncertainty;

What we call strong is really willful imposition.

From a peak of strength there's nowhere to go but down.

Whatever is not in harmony with Dao will come to an early
   end.

Trolling

If Laozi were alive today, he'd be great at Twitter (well, he'd have some competition from Socrates).

Twitter is a platform that excels at misunderstanding. You could go on there and remark that the sky is blue, and some would be outraged that you're not focusing on the green grass crushed under your feet. (Just go look at the replies to tweets from any well-meaning person with a few thousand followers who hasn't learned this lesson about Twitter yet.)

Twitter is fueled by this constant outrage, or "engagement." To be good at Twitter, you have to not care that you'll be misunderstood. To be great at Twitter, you have to not care *and* also say interesting things.

Laozi loves saying interesting things that are easily misunderstood.

Take what he says about babies:

They cry all day without their voice cracking,
For they're at the peak of harmony.

I know what he's getting at, but memories of when my kids were newborns make me grit my teeth. (And, no, telling the anxious and inexperienced parents we were back then that we should "do by not doing" wouldn't have helped either.) Maybe Laozi can give me a lecture on the harmony of babyhood after he's taken care of crying babies for three days with no sleep.

Or what he says about learning:

> To know what happens in the cosmos doesn't require stepping outside the door.
> To understand the ways of heaven doesn't require looking outside the window.

Having devoted so much of my life to schooling, it's hard to suppress the instinct to argue back. In an age when deliberate, active know-nothing ignorance is a point of pride for so many, it's also hard not to think that Laozi could be read to justify the unjustifiable.

Or what he has to say about conventional morality:

> Abandon reverence and calculation, and the people will benefit a hundredfold.
> Cease talk of mercy and justice, and the people will reclaim kindness and goodwill.

Can Laozi be taken literally here? Is this a plausible vision of human nature? I suppose some of us would even laugh at him—*If it's not laughed at, it isn't worthy of being Dao.*

If you want to read Laozi's words uncharitably, you can find fault with every single word of the *Dao De Jing*.

But Laozi doesn't care about uncharitable readings of him. He'll just sit there, pleased as a swallow in his muddy nest or a turtle roaming through the mud, while the people misunderstanding him flop around like fish on land, foaming at the mouth.

As I said, great at Twitter.

My words are easy to understand; my way is easy to follow.
But the world doesn't understand, doesn't follow.

Laozi doesn't think that you can convince anyone of Dao. Words are useless in pinning down what Dao is. All that words can do is shock us out of our daily, mindless wandering, provoke us into seeking the true pattern in the flow of the universe.

He is a troll in the best sense of the word: someone who says things that are meant to sting and shock and irk and annoy and discomfort—but for a purpose beyond mere emotional manipulation, beyond the lulz and the "engagement." Only when we've been jolted out of the conventional, the accepted, the unquestioned, the self-evident, the quotidian ways crafted for our present moment, for our fortuitous place, can we see the deeper patterns, the lasting patterns that form and are formed by Dao.

To know harmony is to know the eternal.
To know the eternal is to achieve clarity.

Chapter 56

THOSE WHO SPEAK, DON'T KNOW

Those who speak, don't know.
Those who know, don't speak.
Block the mind's windows, seal its doors, dull edges, dissolve
    entanglements, hide glows, fuse with terrestrial dust . . .
    these are the ways to ineffable oneness.
Untouched by intimacy,
Untouched by distance,
Untouched by profit,
Untouched by harm,
Untouched by favor,
Untouched by scorn—
That is why all esteem the Dao-aware.

Chapter 57

TO TAKE THE WORLD

The best way to govern a country is to stay on the straight
course of Dao;
The best way to wield an army, on the other hand, is to find
surprising shortcuts;
To take the world, do nothing.
How do I know this?
The more prohibitions, the poorer the population;
The more people arm themselves, the more chaotic the
country;
The more cunning and craft, the more strange events arise;
The more laws, the more lawbreakers.
That is why the Dao-aware say,
"I do nothing, and the people harmonize on their own;
I stay serene, and the people find their own plenty;
I desire nothing, and the people uncarve themselves."

Chapter 58

FORTUNE AND MISFORTUNE

Govern with few words and few deeds, and the people are
 honest and happy.
Govern with sharp words and keen acts, and the people are
 unfulfilled and restless.
Misfortune, fortune relies on you.
Fortune, misfortune hides within you.
Who can tell which is which? There's no certainty.
What is proper can turn strange, and what is good can
 change to ill.
This inconstancy has mystified people since time immemorial.
That is why the Dao-aware are upright but don't oppress,
Keen but don't cut,
Free but don't indulge,
Bright but don't dazzle.

Chapter 59

GATHERING

To administer in accordance with Dao, the most important
act is gathering.
To gather is to be prepared.
To be prepared is to constantly build De.
To stockpile De is to be invincible.
To be invincible is to have inestimable power.
Only then can you be trusted with the nation.
To hold the nation by the source makes it last.
This is the way to be deeply rooted, to endure long and to
see far.

Chapter 60

DEATH CAN CLAIM NO DEVOTION

Guiding a large state is no different from cooking a small fish.

When Dao flows under heaven, death can no longer claim
holy devotion.

No, not just that it can no longer claim devotion, but such
devotion can do no harm.

No, not just such devotion can do no harm, but also the
Dao-aware can do no harm.

When neither the spiritual nor the wise can harm, then De
will return.

Fish

No one can write about death quite the way Zhuangzi does. Here's one of my favorite passages from him:

> The cycle of life and death, like the succession of night and day, is dependent on fate. We can do nothing to intervene in its natural course.
>
> When a spring dries up, the fish who live in it are left on the parched bottom, flopping about, gasping for breath. To stay alive a bit longer, they spit out what little water is left in their mouths to make foam to moisten one another's gills. There is much grandeur in their mutual aid and defiance in the face of death. But if they could . . . wouldn't they prefer to forget, to never know one another, and instead swim freely through lush lakes and surging rivers?
>
> You and I would be better off to forget, to never know about sage kings or cruel tyrants, and let Dao's current bear us away.
>
> The earth holds me up using my fixed form, works me through the trials of living, relaxes me by the decline of senescence, and rests me with the oblivion of death. So if

I think my life is a good thing, I have to think my death is also a good thing.

You can hide a fishing boat in a secluded valley or conceal a mountain inside the boundless ocean—you think your cache is secure, but in the middle of the night a force could still come and take it all away while you, deep asleep, remain unaware.

Only when you hide the world within the world itself do you have true security.

We are pleased when we remain in human form, but the human form is merely one form in the innumerable multitude of forms the cosmos is constantly evolving. The joy in that path of change, of transformation, is impossible to measure.

So the Dao-aware forget themselves and find constancy in change. They roam not Now but Always, not in One form but in All.

Death is good. Senescence is good. The beginning is good. The end is good. You are, like all things in the cosmos, swimming in the flux of Dao.

Chapter 61

TRIUMPH BY STILLNESS

A great state should be like a river flowing down into the sea,
   the world's female core, the gathering of all under heaven.
The female ever triumphs over the male through stillness,
   the stillness of being below.
Thus, a great state that goes below a small state will win
   over the small state;
And a small state that goes below a great state will win over
   the large state.
By submitting, one takes; by staying low, one gathers.
Great states wish to shepherd small states;
Small states wish to ask favors of great states;
Both can have their desires if they hold to being below.

Chapter 62

TREASURED BY THE GOOD . . . AND PRESERVES THE NOT SO GOOD

Dao is the deep mystery of all things in the cosmos.

It's treasured by the good, but also preserves those not so good.

Beautiful words can buy honor; beautiful acts can bring esteem.

How can even those who are not so good be abandoned?

When the emperor ascends to the throne, and the grand ministers are named,

Precious rings of jade are offered before chariots pulled by four horses.

But wouldn't it be better to humbly present the grand path of Dao?

Why have we always valued Dao so? Ha, this is it:

What you desire, Dao will give you.

Where you err, Dao will save you.

Chapter 63

TO SOLVE THE HARD YOU
MUST BEGIN WITH THE EASY

Do by not doing;

Matter by not mattering;

Flavor by not flavoring.

Treat the small as great, the less as more;

Answer an insult with acts of grace.

To solve the hard you must begin with the easy;

To do something big you must start very small.

All difficulties must be resolved through simple steps.

All grand deeds must be performed through tiny details.

Thus the Dao-aware never consider themselves grand, and
     that is why they have grand accomplishments.

Easy promises drain trust; easy words bring many crises.

By seeing everything as difficult, the Dao-aware never have
     difficulties.

Chapter 64

WHERE YOU STAND

Holding what's at rest is simple;
Planning without portents is easy.
The fragile tend to break;
The small tend to scatter.
The doing should happen before there's anything to be done;
The fixing should happen before there's anything to mend.
A tree you can't even wrap your arms around sprouts from a seed;
A sky-tending mound is built from handfuls of earth;
A journey of a thousand miles begins where you stand.

Doing leads to failing; clenching leads to losing.
That is why the Dao-aware don't act and don't fail, don't grasp
    and don't lose.
Often, people stumble when they're almost at the goal. Take the
    same care at the end as at the start, then there will be no fall.
The Dao-aware desire what others don't desire, but disregard what
    others prize;
They study what others don't study, and patch the flaws left by others.
They assist the providence of nature without daring to impose their
    own will.

Chapter 65

WITHOUT CLEVERNESS IS A BLESSING

In ancient times, the Dao-aware did not enlighten the people,
    but left them in their foolishness.
That is because all the people's troubles come from the pro-
    liferation of craft and cunning.
Thus, administering the state with clever stratagems is a
    calamity;
But administering the state without cleverness is a blessing.
To know these two is to know the mold of law;
To know the mold is to know Ineffable De.
Mysterious De reaches profound and far, connecting to the
    return of all things,
To the grand flow of Dao.

Chapter 66

BELOW THEM

Why is the mighty ocean the king of all streams?

Because it lies below all of them.

One who would be above the people must speak from below
them;

One who would lead the people must trail behind them.

The Dao-aware are elevated, but the people don't feel their
weight,

Are foremost, but the people don't fear their power.

The Dao-aware have the lasting support of all.

Because they don't contend, no one contends against them.

Frog in the Well

The ocean is a potent symbol in Daoism. By occupying the lowest spot, it gathers all the world's water. Its freedom and grandeur are hard to comprehend for those bent on their little petty fiefdoms.

Zhuangzi tells the following story about the meaning of the ocean:

Once, there was a frog who lived in a shallow, abandoned well.

One day, while the frog was sunbathing during the single hour of the day when light reached the bottom of the well, he heard a rumbling outside.

"Who's there?" he called. "You're making a lot of noise."

A huge leathery turtle head peeked in over the top of the well. "Sorry! I was just passing by. I'm from the ocean."

"The ocean?" mused the frog, puzzled. "Never heard of it."

The turtle looked down the muddy well, smiling but saying nothing. Then he began to turn away, ready to move on.

"Wait!" said the frog, annoyed that this stranger wasn't impressed by the glimpse he had gotten of the well. "Listen,

I'm a king. Everything you see is my domain. When I want to, I can hop among the bricks lining the well for exercise or sleep in the cracks. When I jump in the water, the waves gently lap the bottom of my chin. When I push my feet into the mud, it yields and covers my toes compliantly. Look about me: all these insects, shrimp, crabs, and tadpoles are my subjects, none of them able to roam about the air, the mud, and the water as freely as I can. Who can claim to be as happy as I? Indeed, I invite you to come in and experience my life a little."

The turtle tried to comply. But the well was so small that he couldn't even get more than one foot into the well. Fearing being trapped, the turtle backed out.

"Listen," said the turtle, "let me tell you about the ocean. It's so broad that I can swim for a thousand days without seeing the shore. It's so deep that even the tallest mountain would be submerged without a trace. In the time of Sage King Yu, there was flooding nine years out of ten, and yet the ocean didn't get any bigger. In the time of King Tang, there was drought seven years out of eight, and yet the ocean never shrank. A second or an eon, the ocean views them the same. Rain or drought, the sea neither increases nor decreases. This is the happiness of the ocean; do you understand?"

The frog, amazed, couldn't pick his jaw out of the mud even long after the turtle was gone.

Chapter 67

THREE TREASURES

People always tell me that Dao is so grand that it's impossible to grasp.

The grandness of Dao is exactly why it isn't like anything.
If it were like anything concrete, it would be too small.

I have three treasures that I hold dear: love, thrift, and never daring to elevate myself.

Because I love, I am brave.

Because I'm thrifty, I can be magnanimous.

Because I never dare to elevate myself, I can be a long-lasting vessel for the flow of the cosmos.

But to abandon love and seek courage, to abandon frugality and seek magnificence, to abandon humbleness and seek advancement . . . that way lies death!

When you hold fast to love, in attack you'll have victory, in defense you'll be invulnerable.

Whatever heaven wishes to save, it protects with love.

Chapter 68

THE DE OF NOT CONTENDING

Good generals are not warlike;

Good warriors are not consumed by fury;

Those with many victories don't seek confrontations;

Those skilled at leading don't look to be exalted.

This is why we speak of the De of not contending and the
power of not controlling.

They are the ancient patterns of Dao.

Chapter 69

ON WAR

Military strategists tell us this:

"I'd rather react than act; I'd rather retreat a mile than advance an inch."

This is called reaching without marching, blocking without arms, confronting without enemies, holding off without weapons.

The worst military error is underestimating the enemy, which almost cost me my dearest treasures.

Thus, if two forces are about equal in strength, the one that takes no delight in war wins.

Chapter 70

WEAR RAGS

My words are easy to understand; my way is easy to follow.

But the world doesn't understand, doesn't follow.

Words have sources; deeds have principles.

Without knowing either, it's impossible to know me.

So few understand me.

Follow me? Even rarer.

The Dao-aware wear rags while holding precious jade.

The Useless Bottle Gourd

It's often said that the Daoists are useless, for their philosophy has no practical application. Dao doesn't give you power, riches, success, the imagined trappings of a good life. In the eyes of detractors, all that Daoists can hope for is a kind of empty, spiritual triumph, a useless sort of pseudofreedom that has no power.

Daoists don't care about critics. But Zhuangzi does tell the following story:

One day, Huizi, one of Zhuangzi's friends, came to visit.

"How have you been, old friend?" asked Zhuangzi.

"Not too great," Huizi said. "The king of Wei gave me some seeds for bottle gourds, which I planted. But when the vines bore fruit, they turned out to be humongous! You want to know how big? Why, each one can hold five buckets of water. If I used one as a container, the walls would burst from the weight of the liquid inside. But if I cut one down the middle to turn each half into a dipper, they'd be so big that there'd be nowhere to fit one in the kitchen. Since I could find no use for them, I had to smash them so they wouldn't take up so much space."

"Ah, you're having trouble making use of big things. That reminds me of a story. In the Spring and Autumn period, there was a family in the state of Song who made a living washing silk. Now, you know that when you work with your hands immersed in cold winter river water all the time, you end up with chapped skin. But this family had an ointment, whose formula was a secret passed down from their ancestors, that kept their hands healthy and smooth no matter how bad the winters were.

"A man then came to the family and offered a hundred pieces of gold for this secret formula. The family got together and discussed the matter.

"'We've been washing silk for many generations. But every year our income is no more than a few pieces of gold. Now we have the chance to get a hundred pieces of gold all at once, for no work! Let's sell the formula to him!'

"The man took the formula and went to the king of Wu, who was about to go to war with the king of Yue. With the help of this ointment, the Wu soldiers were able to fight on winter rivers without fear of chapped hands, and they achieved a great victory over the Yue army. The king of Wu then made the man who brought him the formula a titled noble with his own fief of land.

"Given the same formula, some can only wash silk, but others can win a war. A thing does not have only one use. Here you are, worrying about having no place to store these giant bottle gourds. Why not fill them with air and tie them together as floats for a raft?"

Huizi, however, was unmoved. "Let me tell you about a tall tree in my yard. The trunk is gnarled and twisted, and the branches are full of burrs and deformities. There's no way we can get any good lumber out of it. Indeed, even though it's right by the side of the road, passing carpenters wouldn't even give it a second glance. This tree is just like your speech: grand but useless."

Zhuangzi laughed. "I do enjoy our little debates. All right, let me draw your attention to the weasels who make their home in the fields. They crawl through the grass, close to the ground, pouncing after mice and rabbits. One moment they're here, the next over there; sometimes you see them low, sometimes high. But just as they are enjoying themselves, prancing about, they fall into some hunter's snare and are killed.

"Now, consider the hairy yak, which is so big that when it roams over the grassland some might mistake it for a distant dark cloud. It's capable of many grand deeds. But it's incapable of catching even a single mouse.

"You're telling me that you don't know what to do with this big tree in your yard because you can find no use for it. Why not transplant it somewhere wild? Then, as you wander by on a hike, you can rest in its shade or even take a nap under its canopy. This tree, by your own admission, will never entice anyone to take an axe to it. It has no use for humans, and therefore no harm will come to it. Between you and the tree, who do you think is more free?"

Chapter 71

FAULT

Knowing that you don't know, you're well.

Not knowing but thinking you know, you're ill.

The Dao-aware are faultless because they fault their own faults.

Spots that are spotted are no longer blemishes.

Chapter 72

LIMITLESS

When people stop fearing might, then they become more
than mighty.
They no longer feel constrained by their allotted space;
They no longer fear the bounds of mortality.
By not straining against limits, they become limitless.
The Dao-aware know but don't show, love themselves but
aren't self-important.

Chapter 73

HEAVEN'S NET

Daring based on courage leads to death.

Caution based on courage leads to life.

But that is not always so.

Sometimes providence favors one or the other, and no one
knows why.

Even the Dao-aware find this hard.

Dao does not contend but wins, does not speak but answers,
does not summon but draws.

Deliberate and gradual, it plans for all.

Heaven's net is all-encompassing; its mesh is wide but it
misses nothing.

Chapter 74

WHO SHOULD DEAL DEATH?

When the people don't fear death, they can't be bullied with
　　death threats.
To put the fear of death into the people, I suppose I could
　　seize outsiders and outliers and kill them.
But how dare I?
Death should only be dealt by the master of death.
To usurp that power is akin to taking over the work of a
　　skilled carpenter: rarely does the dunce emerge with all
　　his fingers.

Chapter 75

THE PEOPLE GO HUNGRY

The people go hungry when those above eat too much.
The people are hard to govern when those above crave great
    deeds.
The people care little for lives when those above care too
    much about good living.
That is why dedicating a life to doing nothing is even better
    than prizing life.

Chapter 76

STIFF

In life, your body is supple and pliant; in death, it's stiff as
a board.

In life, grasses and trees are soft and flexible; in death, they're
rigid and withered.

Thus, the hard and tough belong to the realm of the dead,
while the soft and tender belong to the company of the
living.

Powerful armies march to their doom; rigid boughs break
in the storm.

The soft and yielding overcome the strong and powerful.

Chapter 77

DRAWING A BOW

Dao is like drawing a bow.

Too high? Lower it.

Too low? Raise it.

Too far? Relax your arm.

Not enough? Pull harder.

Heaven's way is to take away from too much and make up
for not enough.

But the worldly way is different: it's to take away from not
enough and give to already too much.

What has enough to give to all in the cosmos?

Only Dao.

So the Dao-aware do without preening, achieve without
proclaiming.

Chapter 78

TRUTH OFTEN SOUNDS
LIKE ITS OPPOSITE

The softest, weakest thing in the world is water,

Yet there's nothing better than water at overcoming the tough
and strong.

That weakness wins over strength and softness wins over
hardness are truths everyone knows,

Yet no one can put it into practice.

So the Dao-aware tell us:

"Only one who bears the humiliation of the nation is worthy
of the crown;

Only one who endures the suffering of all can hold the title
of king."

Truth often sounds like its opposite.

Chapter 79

ALWAYS KINDNESS

The draining of great enmity always leaves behind bitter
dregs.

What's the best way out?

The Dao-aware will keep their part of the contract but not
enforce the part held by others.

Replete with De, the focus is on building trust.

Devoid of De, the focus is on exacting what's due.

The way of heaven plays no favorites; it abides always with
kindness.

Not Quite a Postscript

Don't worry. Laozi has more to say. As I didn't start this book with an introduction, it only makes sense to not end it with my words, either. After all, the Book of De didn't always follow the Book of Dao, so why should a postscript always come after the text?

One thing you might have noticed is that as the book went on, there were fewer and fewer personal notes from me. This is a reflection of the process of translation.

It's a common misconception to think that a translation conveys meaning from a language such as "classical Chinese" to another language such as "modern English." In reality, something very different takes place.

Interesting books are not written in abstract, faceless grapholects that subsume innumerable voices under one code, but in deeply personal, sui generis idiolects unique to each author, each tongue, each brush. Melville did not compose *Moby-Dick* in "nineteenth-century English," whatever that means. He wrote it in his own language, with idiosyncratic references, aural patterns, grammatical structures, tropes, images, salty metaphors, sea-shanty litotes, defiant digressions. Neither did Emily Dickinson compose her poems in some lifeless, standard grammar, but infused each dash, each pause for breath, each Capital Letter, with the dance of the bee and the fragrance of the clover, with her inimitable perspective and lived experience.

It's the same with Laozi, who did not write in "classical Chinese," but in his own language—with distinct rhythm, structure, tone, visual puns, a surplus of ideophones, a reliance on paradoxes—discernible even after millennia of edits, emendations, errors.

A worthwhile translation must recognize the essential uniqueness of the source idiolect and then construct a new language just as unique to convey it to a new audience. The *Dao De Jing* is not translated from classical Chinese to modern English, but from Laozi's language to a new language invented by the translator, following tracks left by Laozi.

That invention begins in uncertainty and doubt, with questions, protests, objections. *What do you mean when you say, "By not contending, there can be no error"? Does that mean we shouldn't fight, ever? How can you claim that babies won't be harmed by fierce beasts? What in the world is a straw dog?*

These notes are my way of working these questions out. To create a new language, new words must be defined, new expressions embedded in examples, new styles experimented with. The writer must grow comfortable with the new language and teach it to the reader. (If you are technically inclined, this process is similar to the functions a programmer writes for the library that inevitably coevolves with a new program—much of the work of developing any program is the invention of a unique language of new functions suited to the expression of that program.)

But over time, as the translator constructs the new language to express ideas that once were uncomfortable and new, understanding replaces doubt, improvisation replaces imitation, the broad and open way that is Dao replaces the mazy, circular, circuitous, aimless wanderings of the skeptical mind.

Every good translation should move through the translator as *Paradise Lost* once moved through Milton's mind. What begins as an effort to justify, to explain, to define, ends in willing submission, in a harmonious effort to speak, not *speak for*.

The need to explain, to provide context, to put up signposts, is strongest at the beginning of a translation. These help *both* the writer and the reader to learn the language, to find their own ways.

But over time, I found that I had less and less to say in asides (and the reader also needs them less). Laozi's language, or the language invented by me to convey his, takes over, as it should.

I would be remiss not to acknowledge another reason for there being fewer notes from me in the latter part of the book: choice.

One consequence of studying the *Dao De Jing* that I didn't anticipate is a profound distrust of language. Plato distrusted the written word, but Laozi's distrust of language goes even deeper. Laozi doesn't think much of clever arguments or grand, abstract words that try to stir the soul: benevolence, patriotism, justice, faith, morality. He thinks even less of those who go on and on in the service of these abstractions. He writes beautifully but has nothing but contempt for those who think writing beautifully means the same thing as writing the truth.

I'm haunted by Zhuangzi's image of the foolish prince who treats the words of the sages as wisdom, when they're no more than dead tracks left by the departed dragon, shadows cast by the soaring peng bird.

The more I read of Laozi, the less I wanted to write.

Still, as much as I know that words are not the same as wisdom, I can't help loving Laozi's words. This love is part of my nature, my connection to the flow of energy in the bellows between heaven and earth.

For solace, I return to this chapter again and again.

What's the best way out?
The way of heaven plays no favorites; it abides always with
    kindness.

Heaven and earth are not benevolent. That's why it's even more incumbent upon us to be kind to one another. It's the only way.

Chapter 80

THE IDEAL STATE

Small territory; few people.

Though the people know of engines and instruments, they
don't use them.

Though the people know of distant lands, they value life
and don't roam far.

Though they have ships and carts, they don't ride.

Though they have weapons and armor, they don't war.

They return to the time when tying knots in strings was all
the help memory needed.

The food, delicious; the clothes, beautiful; the houses,
secure; the customs, joyous.

Dogs bark and roosters crow across borders;

The people of neighboring states, however, never meet even
unto death.

Without Intervention

Much of what Laozi has to say about government and leadership is disapproving (at least of the kinds of things that we normally expect governments and leaders to do).

This has not helped with the reception of Daoism by the powerful and ambitious. What could be more odious to them than a philosophy that insists that the greater portion of government is unnecessary and counterproductive, that wars and conquests should be avoided at all costs, that one should always be suspicious of ideologies, big ideas, grand projects that promise to change the world?

It's fair to ask, If government intervention is to be avoided, then how can things ever improve?

Zhuangzi doesn't exactly offer an answer; instead, he tells a story:

A friend asked Laozi, "Without intervention by those with power, how can society improve?"

Laozi replied, "You should be careful about attempts to nudge or direct the hearts of the people. It's our nature to be morose when thwarted, and to be full of pride when indulged. We're prisoners of our passions. To burn like fire when excited, to congeal like ice when depressed, to be deeper than the abyss when still, to be flightier than racing clouds when on the move—there's nothing wilder than the human heart.

"Look back on history. Has there ever been a single wise king or sage lawmaker who managed to 'improve' the human heart one iota? Grand philosophies rise and fall, and this faction or that comes to power, but what are the actual results? Debates, mutual accusations, rationalizations disguised as rationality. Cleverness is prized, and the people compete, contend, fight, over the smallest things. Governments then step in with rules and regulations, punishments and incentives, further disturbing the people's hearts. Even the lords of ten thousand chariots sitting on their thrones tremble with fear.

"Look around you: the bodies of the executed are packed tightly, and the prisons are overflowing. But the Confucians and the Mohists are still out there, debating, accusing, grandstanding, jostling for power, surrounded by shackles and guards. Is there anything more shameless? How do we know that the grand philosophies of sages aren't the bolts on jail doors, or that ideas about benevolence and propriety aren't links in the shackles?

"If we could only end the worship of sages and abandon all ideas deemed clever . . . perhaps then the world will finally see peace."

Chapter 81

DO WITHOUT CONTENDING

Trustworthy words aren't pretty;
Pretty words can't be trusted.
Good people don't argue;
Skilled arguments don't make good people.
Those who know aren't learned.
The well-read don't really know.
The Dao-aware don't hoard, for the more they give to others,
    the more they have.
Heaven's way is to nourish without harm.
The Dao-aware's way is to do without contending.

LIST OF STORIES AND SOURCES

Laozi's Life,《史记·老子韩非列传》

The Wheelwright,《庄子·外篇·天道》

Nightmares,《庄子·外篇·天运》

Pao Ding Carving Cattle,《庄子·内篇·养生主》

The Ideal Leader,《庄子·内篇·应帝王》

On Benevolence,《庄子·外篇·天道》

I Would Rather Drag My Tail through the Mud,
　　《庄子·外篇·秋水》

Laozi's Death,《庄子·内篇·养生主》

The Bird Named Peng and the Fish Named Kun,
　　《庄子·内篇·逍遥游》

Gaining Wisdom,《庄子·外篇·天运》

Fish,《庄子·内篇·大宗师》

Frog in the Well,《庄子·外篇·秋水》

The Useless Bottle Gourd,《庄子·内篇·逍遥游》

Without Intervention,《庄子·外篇·在宥》

ACKNOWLEDGMENTS

I'm grateful to the following individuals for their advice while I worked on this project:

Chen Qiufan, Kate Elliott, Emily Jin, Wang Kanyu.

My agent, Russell Galen, who nurtured the shape of the work.

My international agents, Danny Baror and Heather Baror-Shapiro, who helped me reach more people than I dared to dream.

My editors, Christopher Farley and Kathryn Belden, who helped me find my path beyond cleverness.

Jaya Miceli, for the striking cover, and Kyle Kabel, for the beautiful interior design.

Kassandra Engel, for an extraordinary publicity plan, and Mark Galarrita, for marketing support.

Dan Cuddy, for handling last-minute requests for changes with patience and grace.

The staff at Scribner, for all their assistance during production.

Above all, I thank my wife, Lisa, for her love, support, and strength, and my daughters, Esther and Miranda, for reminding me why all this matters.

ABOUT THE AUTHOR

Ken Liu is an award-winning American author of speculative fiction. His collection *The Paper Menagerie and Other Stories* has been published in more than a dozen languages. Liu's other works include *The Grace of Kings*, *The Wall of Storms*, *The Veiled Throne*, *Speaking Bones*, and a second collection, *The Hidden Girl and Other Stories*. He has been involved in multiple media adaptations of his work including the short story "Good Hunting," adapted as an episode in Netflix's animated series *Love, Death + Robots*; and AMC's *Pantheon*, adapted from an interconnected series of short stories. "The Hidden Girl," "The Message," and "The Cleaners" have also been optioned for development. Liu previously worked as a software engineer, corporate lawyer, and litigation consultant. He frequently speaks at conferences and universities on topics including futurism, creativity in the age of AI, the history of technology, and the value of storytelling. Liu lives with his family near Boston, Massachusetts.